ᐃᓄᒃᑎᑐᑦ ᖃᐅᔨᒪᓕᕐᓇᑏᑦ
inuktitut essentials

A PHRASEBOOK

ᐱᕈᕐᕕᒃ
pirurvik press

ᐃᓄᒃᑎᑐᑦ ᖃᐅᔨᒪᓕᕐᓂᑦ

Inuktitut Essentials: A Phrasebook
1st Edition - April 2009

Published by:

Pirurvik Press
Box 2249
Iqaluit, Nunavut
X0A 0H0
www.pirurvik.ca
info@pirurvik.ca

Editorial Team:

Chris Douglas
Leena Evic
Myna Ishulutak
Gavin Nesbitt
Jeela Palluq

Design and Production: Chris Douglas

External Review: Ooleepika Ikkidluak

ISBN   978 0 9732178 2 7

table of contents

ᓄᕙᓕᐊᑕᕐᖅ

ᓯᕗᓕᐊᑉᑕᖅ
foreword

Inuktitut is both an ancient and a modern language spoken in dozens of Inuit communities that dot the Arctic coastline of eastern North America. In the vast territory known as Nunavut ('our land' in Inuktitut), it is spoken by hunters and lawyers, at community feasts and in the halls of government, by unilingual Elders and children at play.

In the pages of this book, you will get a taste of the specialized terminology that Inuit use to describe our families, our food and our ancient relationship with the Arctic environment. The words and phrases that appear here only touch the surface of a rich lexicon. You will also get a sense of the remarkable ability of the Inuktitut language to evolve in response to the changes that have transformed our way of life. Inside, you will find chapters on computer terms in Inuktitut, how to conduct a telephone conversation or make plans for an evening on the town.

It is our hope that this book will give English speakers the encouragement and confidence they need to use Inuktitut more often in our communities. While there is a growing rate of bilingualism among younger generations, fully 75% of us speak Inuktitut as our mother tongue. Even in the youngest age groups there are many who are able to express themselves most clearly in Inuktitut. Most Nunavummiut over the age of 65 speak no other language.

All of the material in this book appears in *qaniujaaqpait* (syllabics) and *qaliujaaqpait* (roman orthography), the two writing systems that Inuit have used for well over a century. By using the Inuit Cultural Institute's standardized writing system, we have ensured the printed word reflects correct pronunciation.

This has been a collaborative effort, and vocabulary and spellings from various dialects appear on the pages that follow. With few exceptions, the words and expressions we have listed will be understood by fluent speakers of the language throughout Nunavut.

We hope you enjoy this book and welcome your comments.

ABOUT THE AUTHORS

Pirurvik is a centre of excellence for Inuit language, culture and well-being. Founded in the fall of 2003, and based in Iqaluit, Pirurvik has developed a reputation for innovation and quality. Through its team of highly skilled and experienced professionals, Pirurvik offers a range of specialized services, programs and productions.

As an Inuit firm, we are focused on three core concepts:

· Learning what has come before;

· Teaching what is here today; and

· Developing the future vitality of Inuit culture and the Inuktitut language.

The creation of Nunavut in 1999 sparked a renewed effort to protect and advance the use of the Inuktitut language in all aspects of daily life. Pirurvik is committed to developing new opportunities for people to learn and use Inuktitut. Our endeavours are as varied as the partners we work with, including daycares, preschools, Nunavut's francophone community, Inuit and non-profit organizations, government and the private sector.

In addition to our programs, Pirurvik has developed other Inuktitut resources, including text books, a CD of children's music with an accompanying songbook and the award-winning Tusaalanga website (www.tusaalanga.ca).

As an organization built on connecting with Inuit language and culture in all of its richness, our first instinct was to publish a phrasebook of traditional terminology that would revive some of the sophisticated words and expressions that have disappeared from daily speech. Such a resource would give mother tongue speakers of Inuktitut a new appreciation for their language and the cultural legacy that has been passed from one generation to another for centuries.

On the other hand, Pirurvik recognizes the strong desire of many English speakers to learn the Inuit Language. Many have come to the Arctic from elsewhere and are looking to enrich their experience and connection to the Inuit way of life. There is also a growing number of Inuit who have grown up speaking English and who are working to reclaim and enhance their abilities in the language of our ancestors. We see the importance of this reflected in initiatives and legislation designed to support Inuktitut in the workplace and in our education system.

We hope this book marks just the beginning of what will eventually grow into a rich library of resources available to Inuit and non-Inuit alike.

About this phrasebook

Anyone who struggles with the vocabulary and grammar of an unfamiliar language looks for a handy reference that will make sense of it all.

Phrasebooks, of course, cannot teach you another language. If you want to be able to communicate beyond finger pointing and mono-syllabic sentences, there is no substitute for a good course taught by a competent instructor.

Our goal with this phrasebook is to provide Inuktitut learners with some simple and useful words and phrases that can be mastered easily. Keep in mind that fluent speakers of Inuktitut often use much more complex vocabulary and grammar than what appears here.

FINDING WHAT YOU'RE LOOKING FOR

This book is not formatted to slip effortlessly into a back pocket. This is just as well as we don't recommend that you attempt a conversation with a unilingual Elder while frantically flipping through the pages of this book.

Instead, try to prepare ahead of time, researching the expressions you might need during an upcoming conversation. The material is arranged by topic in the front of the book with an Inuktitut-English and English-Inuktitut dictionary on the back pages.

Go to our website www.tusaalanga.ca and listen to the soundfiles so you get the pronunciation and the rhythm of the words right. All of this will help you to communicate successfully (if not elegantly) when the time arises.

DIALECT

As discussed in the following pages, Inuktitut in Nunavut is made up of numerous dialects. Pronunciation and vocabulary can vary considerably. Unfortunately, it isn't possible for us to list all of the terms that could be used depending on the community where you happen to find yourself.

Instead, we have made an effort to include only those terms that can be used across a range of dialects.

Using the phrasebook with our website

This phrasebook contains all the basic elements you need to start learning Inuktitut except one: sound.

For the missing piece of the puzzle, Pirurvik has built a comprehensive website, tusaalanga.ca to complement our books for Inuktitut learners.

Tusaalanga means '*Let me hear*' in Inuktitut. On the website, we post recordings that enable Inuktitut learners to hear correct pronunciation and refine their own.

Tusaalanga includes soundfiles for over 1,000 words and expressions, including the majority of those that appear in this phrasebook.

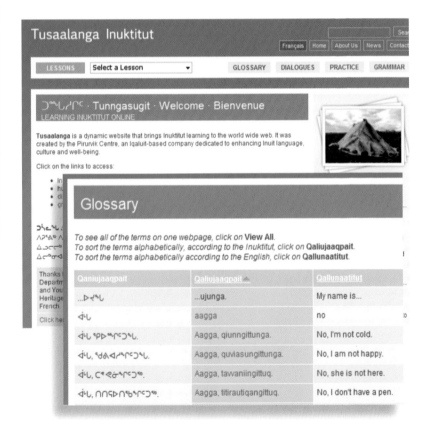

ᐃᓄᒃᑎᑐᑦ
ᐅᖅᑲᐅᓯᑕᓂᐅᑉ
ᒥᒃᓵᓄᑦ

about the Inuktitut language

What is Inuktitut?

This seems like a straightforward question, but it's not. The simplest answer is that Inuktitut is the language spoken by Inuit living in the eastern part of the Canadian Arctic. Approximately 75 percent of Inuit in the territory of Nunavut speak Inuktitut as their mother tongue.

Inuktitut is just one part of what is known as "the Inuit language", spoken from Alaska in the west to Greenland in the east. It might best be understood as a spectrum of dialects that vary enormously from one end of the Arctic to the other. Communities close to one another generally have few problems communicating between dialects, whereas an Alaskan and a Labradorian would have to work at it.

The Inuit Language

Even within Nunavut, vocabulary and pronunciation vary from place to place and between generations. Up until 50 years ago, most Nunavut Inuit lived in isolated camps where distinct speech forms evolved. As they settled into permanent communities, speakers of varying dialects often became neighbours in the same hamlet. This mixing has intensified with the modern-day migration of Inuit in search of employment and opportunities in other communities.

Daily life helps break down communication barriers. So, too, does media, like CBC (Canada's national radio and television broadcaster), by exposing Inuktitut speakers to a range of dialects spoken throughout the territory. Today, fluent speakers in all parts of Nunavut can normally understand each other with only minor difficulties.

How many Inuktitut dialects are there? Among Inuit, as well as among linguists there is no consensus. Nonetheless, most would group the different forms of speaking Inuktitut in Nunavut along these lines:

Inuinnaqtun	Qurluqtuq (Kugluktuk) Iqaluktuuttiaq (Cambridge Bay) Ulukhaqtuq (Ulukhaktok) in the Northwest Territories.
Natsilingmiut	Uqhuqtuuq (Gjoa Haven) Talurjuaq (Taloyoak) Kuugaarjuk (Kugaaruk)
Aivilingmiut	Naujaat (Repulse Bay) Igluligaarjuk (Chesterfield Inlet) Salliq (Coral Harbour)
Kivalliq	Qamani'tuaq (Baker Lake) Kangiqłiniq (Rankin Inlet) Tikirarjuaq (Whale Cove) Arviat
Qikiqtaaluup uannangani / North Baffin	Ikpiarjuk (Arctic Bay) Mittimatalik (Pond Inlet) Iglulik (Igloolik) Sanirajaq (Hall Beach) Qausuittuq (Resolute) Aujuittuq (Grise Fiord)
Qikiqtaaluup kanannanga/ Central Baffin	Kangiqtugaapik (Clyde River) Qikiqtarjuaq Panniqtuuq (Pangnirtung)
Qikiqtaaluup nigiani / South Baffin	Iqaluit Kimmirut Kinngait (Cape Dorset)
Nunavik	the communities of Arctic Quebec and, in Nunavut : Sanikiluaq Aujuittuq (Grise Fiord) and Qausuittuq (Resolute)

Differences between dialects

VOCABULARY

The Inuktitut dialects spoken in Nunavut share the vast majority of their vocabulary. Nonetheless, among them there are some striking differences in very common terminology:

	no	thank you
Inuinnaqtun	imannaq	quana
Natsilingmiut	iiq	qujanaq
Kivalliq	nauk	ma'na
N. Baffin	aakka	qujannamiik
S. Baffin	aagga	nakurmiik /qujannamiik

AFFIXES

In terms of vocabulary, the biggest differences among dialects are in their use of affixes. This can pose particular challenges for Inuktitut learners. Louis Jacques Dorais' *Inuit Languages and Dialects* (Nunavut Arctic College 2003) is an excellent place to begin with lists of affixes in a number of Canadian dialects.

PRONUNCIATION

Where Inuktitut dialects vary most is in the area of pronunciation.

S vs. H

As a general rule, the same words that in eastern Nunavut are pronounced with an **S** are pronounced with an **H** sound in the west :

ili**h**aiji	ili**s**aiji	*teacher*
havik	**s**avik	*knife*
i**h**umajuq	i**s**umajuq	*he thinks*

Speakers of the Natsilingmiut dialect use the **H** sound, as do speakers of Inuinnaqtun. All Qikiqtaaluk (Baffin) dialects use the **S** sound. Speakers of the Kivalliq dialect may use **S** or **H** in different situations.

The syllabic writing system tries to minimize this difference by using the same character (ⲟ ⲟ ⲏ) for both pronunciations.

So the Inuktitut name for Gjoa Haven

ᐅᖅᓱᖅᑑᖅ

would be pronounced Uq**s**uqtuuq in eastern Nunavut and Uh̲uqtuuq in the western part of the territory.

DOUBLE CONSONANTS

Inuktitut learners will notice that some dialects use double consonants much more than others. Nunavut's western dialects very seldom use double consonants. Instead, you will see a wide range of consonants put together. To demonstrate just a few :

i**lv**it	*you*
up**l**aaq	*morning*
ug**j**uk	*bearded seal*
ap**q**ut	*road*

Speakers of Nunavut's eastern dialects, meanwhile, tend to merge many of these pairs of consonants together when they speak. In doing so, the first consonant twins iteslf with the second, resulting in a double consonant.

So instead of:

tu**kt**u	ug**j**uk	qi**nm**iq

we get:

tu**tt**u	u**jj**uk	qi**mm**iq

Generally, you will encounter more double consonants in the Inuktitut language, as you move from west to east across the Canadian Arctic. Within Nunavut, Inuktitut speakers in Panniqtuuq probably use double consonants most often, while speakers of Inuinnaqtun the least. Between the two extremes, some dialects will use double consonants in some situations but not in others :

	Kivalliq	North Baffin	S.&C. Baffin
caribou	tuktu	tuktu	tuttu
Did she go out?	anilauqpa?	anilauqpa?	anilauqqa
road	apqut	aqqut	aqqut
when we saw	takugapta	takugatta	takugatta

9

TS / SS / TS / PS / FF

A very common difference among dialects occurs around these combinations of consonants. Generally, where one dialect will use one pair of consonants, other dialects will consistently substitute another pair of consonants. If you figure out the pattern each dialect follows, you should be able to navigate your way through the variety of spellings that are often used for the same word in Inuktitut.

poisson séché

pit**si**	Qikiqtaaluup nigiani (South Baffin)
pis**si**	Qikiqtaaluup uannangani/kanannanga (North & Central Baffin)
pip**si**	Aivilik
pip**hi**	Natsilingmiut, Kivalliq
pip**hi** / pif**fi***	Inuinnaqtun

*Although **ff** is commonly used by Inuinnaqtun speakers, it is not recognized in the ICI standardized writing system. The standardized spelling would be **ph**.

SPECIAL SOUNDS

There are several sounds that are unique to specific dialects.

ɬi, ɬu ,ɬa (ᑦ, ᑐ ,ᖦ)

This is a sound made by putting the tip of your tongue on the roof of the mouth and blowing air over the sides of the tongue. Speakers of North Baffin, Natsilingmiut, Aivilik and Kivalliq dialects make this sound. As for speakers of Nunavut's other dialects, not only is this sound absent from their speech, they often have great difficulty pronouncing it. Instead, they substitute other consonants in place of the ɬi, ɬu ,ɬa sound.

rope

akɬunaaq	Qikiqtaaluup uannangani (North Baffin)
attunaaq	Qikiqtaaluup nigiani/kanannanga (S. & Cen. Baffin)
akhunaaq	Inuinnaqtun

THE RETROFLEX J (ɟ)

One dialect, Natsilingmiut, also uses a retroflex consonant, which is similar to the R sound used in English. It is heard in places where other dialects would use a **J** sound.

Linguists will often write this sound as **ɟ**. It is also sometimes written as rj. in roman orthography.

i**ɟ**i	ug**ɟ**uk	Kuugaa**ɟ**uk
eye	*bearded seal*	*Kugaaruk (Pelly Bay)*

When the writing system for Inuktitut was standardized in the 1970s, this sound was overlooked and no syllabic character created for it. This causes problems for Natsilingmiut speakers when writing their dialect.

B

B is a sound that is heard throughout the Kivalliq and Qitirmiut (Kitikmeot) regions. Speakers of these dialects will use it where some Inuinnaqtun speakers will use a **p** or a **v**. Speakers of Qikiqtaaluk dialects do not make this sound and use a double consonant instead.

	Inuinnaqtun	Kivalliq	Qikiqtaaluk
eyebrow	qaplu/qablu	qablu	qallu
morning	uplaaq/ublaaq	ublaaq	ullaaq

Although many Nunavummiut use the **b** when writing in roman orthography, this letter was not included in the ICI standardized writing system. The standardized spelling of this sound uses a **p** or a **v**. In standardized syllabics, the two words above are written:

ᖃᕝᓗ / ᖃᑉᓗ　　ᐅᑉᓛᖅ

Glottal Stop

The glottal stop is a little catch in the back of the throat that temporarily stops the flow of air coming from the lungs. An example where English speakers make this sound is between the syllables in the expression « uh-oh ».

Speakers of the Kivalliq and Natsilingmiut dialects make this sound, although it only appears in a small number of words, including :

ma'na	*thank you*
Qamani'tuaq	*Baker Lake*

about Inuktitut

FINAL N or NG

When the syllabic and roman writing systems for Inuktitut were standardized in the 1970s, it was agreed that words could only end with a vowel or with one of three consonants: **q**, **k** or **t** (and, occassionally, with **p** or **m**).

In practice, though, many Inuktitut speakers have a tendency to pronounce these final consonants as an **N** or an **NG** sound. This can be a generational difference as Inuit elders are more likely to do this than younger speakers.

This tendency spills over into the written language. Many Inuinnaqtun speakers will end words with a written **N**. In syllabics, although one may see words ending in ᓇ or ᖕ it is generally discouraged among educators and language professionals.

Writing Inuktitut

Apart from their Siberian cousins, Inuit across the circumpolar world use two types of orthography to write their language. The roman or Latin alphabet is the only writing system used in Alaska, the Northwest Territories, Labrador and in Greenland. This is also the case in Nunavut's Inuinnaqtun speaking communities. Everywhere else in Nunavut and in Nunavik, a unique and easily recognized writing system, known as syllabics is predominant although roman letters are sometimes used as well.

Both the syllabic and roman writing systems for Inuktitut were originally developed by Christian missionaries who needed a way to write the bible, hymns and other printed texts in Inuktitut. Syllabic orthography, in particular, was easy for Inuktitut-speakers to learn. Inuit trained in syllabics were able to pass along their new skills to others so that writing reached some areas of Nunavut before missionaries managed to get there.

Missionaries working in different areas and for different churches, developed their own unique ways of writing with syllabic and roman characters. By the 1960s this was creating problems in printing Inuktitut materials for a wide audience.

In 1976, the Inuit Cultural Institute (ICI) approved a new standardized writing system that could be used to write Inuktitut consistently. ICI orthography has two forms, one in roman orthography (using the Latin alphabet) and one in syllabics. In Inuktitut these are known respectively as *qaliujaaqpait* and *qaniujaaqpait*. The syllabic and roman forms of the ICI system mirror each other so that it is easy to convert text from one to the other.

INUIT CULTURAL INSTITUTE (ICI)
STANDARDIZED ORTHOGRAPHY

	Δ i	▷ u	◁ a	naniit
p	∧ pi	> pu	< pa	‹ p
t	∩ ti	⊃ tu	⊂ ta	⊂ t
k	ρ ki	ժ ku	b ka	ᙂ k
g	ᒋ gi	J gu	ᒐ ga	ᒡ g
m	Γ mi	⌐ mu	L ma	ᒻ m
n	σ ni	ᓄ nu	ᓇ na	ᓐ n
s/h	ᓯ si/hi	ᓱ su/hu	ᓴ sa/ha	ᔅ s
l	⊂ li	⊃ lu	ᓚ la	ᓪ l
j	ᔨ ji	ᔪ ju	ᔭ ja	ᔾ j
v	ᕕ vi	ᕗ vu	ᕙ va	ᕝ v
r	ᕆ ri	ᕈ ru	ᕋ ra	ᕐ r
q	ᖀ qi	ᖁ qu	ᖃ qa	ᖅ q
ng	ᖏ ngi	ᖑ ngu	ᖓ nga	ᖕ ng
ł	ᖠ łi	ᖢ łu	ᖤ ła	ᖦ ł

The syllabic writing system

While roman orthography is frequently used by Inuktitut speakers, the ability to read syllabics is essential in most of Nunavut.

The syllabic system is quite easy to master. Learners are usually able to decipher and begin using the characters with a little practice.

Referring to the chart on the previous page, note that each syllabic character represents an entire syllable (normally a consonant followed by a vowel), hence the name of the writing system.

Inuktitut has 14 consonants, each represented by a particular syllabic character. That character is then rotated clockwise or reversed to represent Inuktitut's three core vowel sounds, **i**, **u** and **a**:

Γ = m + i   ⌐ = m + u   L = m + a

σ = n + i   ⌐o = n + u   α = n + a

When a vowel is not preceded by a consonant, one of the following syllabic characters is used:

Δ (i)   ▷ (u)   ◁ (a)

Δˢbᴶᴦ▷Cˢb   Iqalummiutaq   *resident of Iqaluit*

When a consonant is not followed by a vowel, special characters known as *naniit,* or "finals" are used. Finals are smaller characters that appear in superscript.

ᴸΓ = mmi

Children learning how to write syllabics are said to be learning their "i, pi, ti's". They memorize each column going down (i, pi, ti, gi, mi, ni, etc.). If you keep this in mind, you will quickly see, the **i** characters have a vertical orientation, the **u** characters tend to point to the right and the **a** characters to the left.

Vowel sounds are often lengthened (drawn out) in Inuktitut. These sounds are represented by a dot that is placed above the syllabic character. In *qaliujaaqpait* (roman orthography), these sounds are represented by double vowels.

αdˢΓˢb   nakurmiik   *thank you*

Generally, no more than two vowels can appear in a row. The same holds for consonants - no more than two can appear in a row. When writing Inuktitut words, two finals never appear together.

QUIRKY CHARACTERS

Pay attention to a few syllabic characters that look like a final plus another character, but are in fact a single character:

ᖅ	qi
ᖁ	qu
ᖃ	qa
ᖏ	ngi
ᖑ	ngu
ᖓ	nga

Although **ng** looks like two consonants in roman orthography, linguistically, it is considered one.

When **ng** is doubled, it is written **nng** in roman orthography and like this in syllabics:

ᙱ	nngi
ᙲ	nngu
ᙳ	nnga

ᐱᙳᐊᕐᕕᒃ   pinnguarvik   *recreation centre*

Another tricky character is a double **q** sound. In Nunavut, this sound is written:

ᖅᑭ	qqi
ᖅᑯ	qqu
ᖅᑲ	qqa

ᓄᖅᑲᕆᑦ   Nuqqarit!   *Stop!*

In syllabics, the roman letter **H** is inserted for certain words borrowed from English:

Hᐊᑭ   haaki   *hockey*

Pronunciation

VOWELS

There are three basic vowel sounds in Inuktitut, represented by the letters **i**, **u**, and **a** in *qaliujaaqpait.*

kisu	i**l**lu	nu**n**a

Each of these vowels has a range of sounds it can make in a particular word. Listen for a softer sounding vowel when it appears before the letters **q** or **r**:

iqaluit	**ir**niq	**im**iq
uqaq	Qur**l**uqtuq	

Long vowels are pronounced as above, except that the sound is drawn out so that it is twice as long:

ii	nakurm**ii**k
aa	at**aa**ta

Vowels can also be used in combination:

au	**au**llaqtuq
ai	iiq**ai**
ia	ni**a**quq
iu	ni**u**virvik
ui	t**ui**

Remember that as a general rule, no more than two vowels or two consonants can appear in a row.

CONSONANTS

These letters in Inuktitut are pronounced similarly to English:

p	**t**	**k**	**g**	**m**
n	**s**	**l**	**v**	**ng**

The following letters are pronounced differently than in English:

j　　is pronounced like the English **y** in the word *yak*

r　　This sound is not made in English but is similar to the way **r** is pronounced in French or the **j** in Spanish. It sounds like a slight gargle at the back of the throat.

q　　Another sound produced at the back of the throat. To begin, close your throat with the very back of your tongue, as if you were about to pronounce a **g**. Release air as if you were pronouncing a **k**.

ł　　Put your tongue in the same position as you would to pronounce an **l**. Without using your vocal cords, breathe out, as if you were pronouncing an **sh**.

jj　　Sounds like a **d** + **j**

All other double consonants are drawn out, so that the sound is twice as long.

The basic structure of Inuktitut

In English, the basic unit of meaning is the word. Each word (generally) expresses a separate idea:

> *The dog sleeps under the tree.*

Inuktitut features much longer words, which often would require a whole sentence to express in English.

> qangatasuukkuvimmuuriaqalaaqtunga
>
> *I'll have to go to the airport.*

There are two basic units of meaning in Inuktitut: roots and affixes.

Roots involve basic vocabulary and always appear at the beginning of words in Inuktitut. Here are some examples:

niri-	*to eat*
aullaq-	*to leave town*
tupiq	*tent*

Affixes are attached to the end of roots and other affixes. They can never begin a word. Here are three simple affixes:

-tunga	*I*
-tutit	*you*
-tuq	*she or he*

If we add these affixes to the same root, we get different meanings:

aullaq**tunga**	*I leave*
aullaq**tutit**	*you leave*
aullaq**tuq**	*she / he leaves*

Inuktitut words get built up like a train. Many different affixes can be added to the same root. For example, if we add the affix **–lauq** which marks the past tense, we would get:

aulla**lauq**tunga	*I left*
aulla**lauq**tutit	*you left*
aulla**lauq**tuq	*he / she left*

ᐱᔪᓐ ᐊᑭᓴᑐᑦ
basics

survival inuktitut
colours & numbers
motion & direction
time

ᐱᓴᓇᐊᑭᑦᑐᑦ

survival inuktitut

ᐄ	ii	*yes*
ᐋᒡᒐ	aagga	*no (S. Baffin)*
ᐋᒃᑲ	aakka	*no (N. Baffin)*
ᐋᑦᓲ	aatsuu	*I don't know.*
ᐃᒻᒪᖅᑲ	immaqa	*maybe*
ᐅᕝᕙᓘᓐᓃᑦ	uvvaluunniit	*or*
ᐊᒻᒪᓗ	ammalu	*and*
ᒥᑦᓵᓄᑦ	mitsaanut	*about*
ᑭᓯᐊᓂ	kisiani	*but*
ᐋᒡᒐ ᓱᓕ	aagga suli	*not yet*
ᐃᓛᓐᓂᒃᑯᑦ	ilaannikkut	*sometimes*
ᒫᓐᓇ	maanna	*now*
ᒪᒥᐊᓇᖅ	mamianaq	*sorry*
ᓇᑯᕐᒦᒃ	nakurmiik	*thank you (S. Baffin)*
ᖁᔭᓐᓇᒦᒃ	qujannamiik	*thank you (N. Baffin)*
ᒪ'ᓇ	ma'na	*thank you (Kivalliq)*
ᖁᐊᓇ	quana	*thank you (Inuinnaqtun)*
ᐃᓛᓕ	ilaali	*you're welcome*
ᐃᕝᕕᓪᓕ?	ivvilli?	*and you? (1 person)*
ᐃᓕᑦᓯᓪᓕ?	ilitsilli?	*and you two?*
ᐃᓕᑦᓯᓕ?	ilitsili?	*and you? (3 or more)*
ᐅᕙᖓ	uvanga	*I; me*
ᐅᕙᒍᒃ	uvaguk	*we; us (2)*
ᐅᕙᒍᑦ	uvagut	*we; us (3 or more)*
ᐃᕝᕕᑦ	ivvit	*you (1)*
ᐃᓕᑦᓯᒃ	ilitsik	*you (2)*
ᐃᓕᑦᓯ	ilitsi	*you (3 +)*

ᐅᓇ	una	*this*
ᐅᑯᐊ	ukua	*these*
ᓱᒻᒪᑦ?	summat?	*why?*
ᑭᓇ?	kina?	*who?*
ᖃᖓ?	qanga?	*when?*
ᖃᓄᖅ?	qanuq?	*how?*
ᓇᒥ?	nami?	*where?*
ᐊᒥᓱᑦ	amisut	*lots, many*
ᐊᒥᓲᙱᑦᑐᑦ	amisuunngittut	*few; not many*
ᒥᑭᔪᒥᒃ	mikijumik	*a little bit*
ᑭᖑᓪᓕᖅᐹᖅ	kingulliqpaaq	*the last one*
ᓯᕗᓪᓕᖅᐹᖅ	sivulliqpaaq	*the first one*
ᐊᔾᔨᒌᒃ	ajjigiik	*They (2) are the same.*
ᐊᔾᔨᒌᙱᑦᑑᒃ	ajjigiinngittuuk	*They (2) are different.*
ᐊᖏᔪᖅ	angijuq	*big*
ᒥᑭᔪᖅ	mikijuq	*small*
ᑕᑭᔪᖅ	takijuq	*tall*
ᓇᐃᑦᑐᖅ	naittuq	*short*
ᐱᐅᔪᖅ	piujuq	*good*
ᐱᐅᓂᖅᓴᖅ	piuniqsaq	*better*
ᖃᐅᓯᖅᑐᖅ	qausiqtuq	*wet*
ᐸᓂᖅᑐᖅ	paniqtuq	*dry*
ᓱᒃᑲᐃᑦᑐᖅ	sukkaittuq	*slow*
ᓱᒃᑲᔪᖅ	sukkajuq	*fast*
ᐅᕿᑦᑐᖅ	uqittuq	*light*
ᐅᖁᒪᐃᑦᑐᖅ	uqumaittuq	*heavy*
ᑎᓯᔪᖅ	tisijuq	*hard*
ᐊᕿᑦᑐᖅ	aqittuq	*soft*
ᖃᓂᑦᑐᖅ	qanittuq	*near; close*
ᐅᖓᓯᑦᑐᖅ	ungasittuq	*far*
ᐃᓗᐊᓂ	iluani	*inside*
ᓯᓚᒥ	silami	*outside*

asking for help

ᓱᕙ?
Suva?
What?

Hᐊᐃ?
hai?
What?

ᓱᕙᒎᖅ?
Suvaguuq?
What did he/she say?

ᖃᓄᕉᖅ?
Qanuruuq?
How was that again?

ᐅᖃᒃᑲᓐᓂᕈᒃ
Uqakkanniruk
Please repeat that.

ᑐᑭᓯᙱᑦᑐᖓ
Tukisinngittunga.
I don't understand.

ᑐᑭᓯᑦᑎᐊᖏᑦᑐᖓ
tukisittiangittunga
I don't really understand.

ᐊᔪᓕᕋᒪ
Ajulirama
I'm lost (I've come to the end of my ability).

ᓇᓗᓕᕋᒪ
Nalulirama
I'm confused.

ᐃᓕᓐᓂᐊᑐᐃᓐᓇᖅᑐᖓ
Ilinniatuinnaqtunga
I'm only just learning.

ᓱᒃᑲᐃᓪᓗᑎᑦ ᐅᖃᕈᒃ.
Sukkaillutit uqaruk.
Say it slowly.

ᐅᖃᒃᑲᓐᓂᑲᐃᓐᓇᕆᑦ
uqakkannikainnarit
Please say it again.

ᖃᓄᖅ ᐅᓇ ᑐᑭᖃᖅᐸ?
Qanuq una tukiqaqpa?
What does this mean?

ᖃᓄᖅ ᐅᖃᖅᑕᐅᓲᖑᕙ?
qanuq uqaqtausuunguva?
How is it pronounced?

ᐅᖃᑦᑎᐊᕋᓱᑦᑐᖓ.
Uqattiarasuttunga.
I'm trying to say it properly.

ᖃᓄᖅ . . . ᑐᑭᖃᖅᐸ?
Qanuq . . . tukiqaqpa?
What does . . . mean?

ᐅᓇ ᑭᓲᕙ?
Una kisuuva?
What is this?

ᐅᑯᐊᒃ ᓱᓇᐅᕚᒃ?
Ukuak kisuuvaak?
What are these two things?

ᐅᑯᐊ ᑭᓲᕙᑦ?
Ukua kisuuvat?
What are these?

in conversation: introductions

>> ᑭᓇᐅᕕᑦ?
Kinauvit?
What's your name?

... ᐅᔪᖓ / ... ᖑᔪᖓ
... ujunga / ... ngujunga «
My name is ...

>> ᑭᓇᐅᕙ?
Kinauva?
What is his / her name?

ᐅᓇ ...
Una ... «
This is ...

>> ᓇᒥᒥᐅᑕᐅᕕᑦ?
Namimiutauvit?
Where are you from;
Where do you live?

ᐃᖃᓗᒻᒥᐅᑕᐅᔪᖓ
Iqalummiutaujunga «
I'm from Iqaluit;
I live in Iqaluit

ᒫᓂᒥᐅᑕᐅᔪᖓ.
Maanimiutaujunga.
I'm from here.

>> ᓇᒥᒥᐅᑕᐅᕙ?
Namimiutauva?
Where is she/he from;
Where does she/he live?

ᐊᑐᕚᒥᐅᑕᖅ
Aatuvaamiutaq «
She/he's from Ottawa.
She/he lives in Ottawa

>> ᓇᒥᒥᐅᑉᓴᔭᐅᕕᑦ?
namimiussajauvit?
Where are you originally
from?

ᐸᓐᓂᖅᑑᕐᒥᐅᑉᓴᔭᐅᔪᖓ.
Panniqtuurmiussajaujunga. «
I'm originally from
Pangnirtung.

>> ᐃᓄᒃᑎᑑᓲᖑᕕᑦ?
inuktituusuunguviit?
Do you speak Inuktitut?

ᐃᓄᒃᑎᑑᓲᖑᔪᖓ.
Inuktituusuungujunga. «
I speak Inuktitut.

>> ᖃᓪᓗᓇᐅᔭᓲᖑᕕᑦ?
qallunaujasuunguvit?
Do you speak English?

ᒥᑭᔪᒥᒃ.
Mikijumik. «
A little bit.

>> ᐅᐃᕖᑎᑑᓲᖑᕕᑦ?
uiviitituusuunguvit?
Do you speak French?

ᐃᐳᓚᐃᒃ.
iigalaak. «
A little.

ᐊᒥᐊᑦ ᓈᓴᐅᑎᑦ
colours & numbers

ᐊᒥᐊᑦ	amiat	*colours*
ᐊᐅᐸᔮᖓᔪᖅ	aupajaangajuq	*orange*
ᐊᐅᐸᖅᑐᖅ	aupaqtuq	*red*
ᑲᔪᖅ	kajuq	*brown*
ᑐᖓᔪᖅᑐᖅ	tungujuqtuq	*blue*
ᐃᑦᑎᙳᐊᖅ	ittinnguaq	*purple*
ᖁᖅᓱᖅᑐᖅ	quqsuqtuq	*yellow*
ᓯᐊᕐᓇᖅ	siarnaq	*grey*
ᖃᑯᖅᑐᖅ	qakuqtuq	*white*
ᕿᕐᓂᖅᑐᖅ	qirniqtuq	*black*
ᐆᔭᐅᔭᖅ	uujaujaq	*green*

IN CONTEXT

The words used for colours and numbers in Nunavut vary considerably from region to region. The ones presented here are from North Qikiqtaaluk (Baffin).

Traditional numbers are used frequently in conversation, especially the numbers 1 to 5. For numbers above 10, and when talking about money, time, or phone numbers, Inuktitut speakers are more likely to use terms borrowed from English and adapted to their pronunciation.

inuktitut numbers

ᓈᓴᐅᑎ	naasauti	*number*
ᐊᑕᐅᓯᖅ	atausiq	*one*
ᒪᕐᕉᒃ	marruuk	*two*
ᐱᖓᓱᑦ	pingasut	*three*
ᓯᑕᒪᑦ; ᑎᓴᒪᑦ	sitamat; tisamat	*four*
ᑕᓪᓕᒪᑦ	tallimat	*five*
ᐱᖓᓲᔪᖅᑐᑦ	pingasuujuqtut	*six*
ᓯᑕᒪᐅᔪᙱᒐᖅᑐᑦ	sitamaujunngigaqtut	*seven*
ᓯᑕᒪᐅᔪᖅᑐᑦ	sitamaujuqtut	*eight*
ᖁᓕᐅᙱᒐᖅᑐᑦ	quliunngigaqtut	*nine*
ᖁᓕᑦ	qulit	*ten*
ᐊᕙᑎᑦ	avatit	*twenty*

borrowed numbers

ᔾᐅᓗ	jiulu	*zero*
ᐅᐊᓐ	uan	*one*
ᑐ	tuu	*two*
ᑕᓕ	talii	*three*
ᐳᐊ	pua	*four*
ᐸᐃ	pai	*five*
ᓴᓯ	sassi	*six*
ᓴᐃᐸᓐ	saipan	*seven*
ᐃᑦ	iit	*eight*
ᓇᐃᓐ	nain	*nine*
ᑕᔭᓐ	tajan	*ten*
ᐃᓕᐊᐸᓐ	iliapan	*eleven*
ᑐᐊᔪ	tuaju	*twelve*

ᓄᖅᑲᕆᑦ
STOP
photo: Sébastien Lap

ᖃᓄᐃᓕᐅᖅᐸ, ᓱᑯᑦᑎᐊᓃᑉᐸ
motion & location

ᓱᒃᑲᐃᑦᑐᖅ	sukkaittuq	*slow*
ᓱᒃᑲᔪᖅ	sukkajuq	*fast*
ᓄᖅᑲᖓᔪᖅ	nuqqangajuq	*still; motionless*
ᑕᓕᖅᐱᒃ	taliqpik	*right*
ᓴᐅᒥᒃ	saumik	*left*
ᐅᖓᓯᑦᑐᖅ	ungasittuq	*far*
ᖃᓂᑦᑐᖅ	qanittuq	*close*
ᐊᑭᐊᓃᑦᑐᖅ	akianiittuq	*it's on the other side*
ᐊᑖᓃᑦᑐᖅ	ataaniittuq	*it's underneath*
ᖄᖓᓃᑦᑐᖅ	qaanganiittuq	*it's on top of*
ᖁᓛᓃᑦᑐᖅ	qulaaniittuq	*it's above*
ᓵᖓᓃᑦᑐᖅ	saanganiittuq	*it's in front of*
ᓴᓂᐊᓃᑦᑐᖅ	sanianiittuq	*it's beside*
ᓯᓈᓃᑦᑐᖅ	sinaaniittuq	*it's at the edge of*
ᓯᕗᕌᓃᑦᑐᖅ	sivuraaniittuq	*it's in front of*
ᑐᓄᐊᓃᑦᑐᖅ	tunuaniittuq	*it's behind*
ᐅᖓᑖᓃᑦᑐᖅ	ungataaniittuq	*it's at the back of*
ᓯᓚᑖᓃᑦᑐᖅ	silataaniittuq	*it's outside of*
ᐃᓗᐊᓃᑦᑐᖅ	iluaniittuq	*it's inside of*
ᐊᑯᓐᓂᖓᓃᑦᑐᖅ	akunninganiittuq	*it's between*

ᐊᕐᒡᑦᑐᖕᖕᓇᖅᐱᑦ?
Aquttunnaqpit?
Do you know how to drive?

ᐊᕐᒡᑦᑐᖕᖕᓇᖅᑐᖕᒐ.
Aquttunnaqtunga.
I know how to drive.

ᓄᓇᓯᐆᖅᑐᖅ
nunasiuqtuq
He is driving a car.

ᖃᒧᑕᐅᔭᖅᑐᖅ
qamutaujaqtuq
She is driving a skidoo.

ᐆᒥᐊᖅᑐᖅᑐᖕᒐ.
Umiaqtuqtunga.
I am driving a boat.

ᑐᑭᓕᐊᕐᓗᑎᑦ
Tukiliarlutit
Go straight.

ᑐᐊᕕᓚᐅᕆᑦ!
Tuavilaurit!
Hurry up!

ᑐᐊᕕᕆᐊᖃᓕᖅᑐᖕᒐ.
Tuaviriaqaliqtunga
I have to hurry.

ᓱᒃᑲᐃᒋᐊᓚᐅᕆᑦ! / ᑲᑦᑐᕆᐊᕆᑦ!
Sukkaigialaurit! / Katturiarit!
Slow down!

ᓄᖅᑲᕆᑦ!
Nuqqarit!
Stop!

ᑕᓕᖅᐲᒻᒧᑦ ᓴᖑᓗᑎᑦ.
Taliqpimmut sangulutit.
Turn right.

ᓴᐆᒻᒧᑦ ᓴᖑᓗᑎᑦ.
Saumimmut sangulutit.
Turn left.

ᐱᓱᒃᑐᖅ
pisuktuq
He / she walks.

ᐅᑦᓚᒃᑐᖅ
ullaktuq
He / she runs.

ᕿᒡᒋᖅᑕᖅᑐᖅ
qiggiqtaqtuq
He / she is jumping.

ᐃᖃᐃᓕᓴᖅᑐᖅ
iqailisaqtuq
She / he is exercising.

ᐹᑦᓚᒃᑐᖅ
paallaktuq
He / she stumbles.

ᐅᕙᓃᑦᑐᖅ
uvaniittuq
It's right here.

ᒫᓃᑦᑐᖅ
maaniittuq
It's around here.

ᑕᐅᕙᓃᑦᑐᖅ
tauvaniittuq
It's over there (general area)

ᑕᐃᑲᓃᑦᑐᖅ
taikaniittuq
It is over there (specific spot)

ᑕᐅᓇᓃᑦᑐᖅ
taunaniittuq
It is down there.

in conversation: location

>> **ᓇᒦᑉᐹ?**
Namiippa?
Where is it?

ᒫᓃᑦᑐᖅ. <<
Maaniittuq.
It's here.

ᑕᐅᕙᓃᑦᑐᖅ.
Tauvaniittuq.
It's around there.

ᐃᒪᐅᑉ ᖃᓂᒋᔮᓃᑦᑐᖅ.
Imaup qanigijaaniittuq.
It's by the sea.

ᑐᐱᐅᑉ ᖃᓂᒋᔮᓃᑦᑐᖅ.
Tupiup qanigijaaniittuq.
It's by the tent.

>> **ᓱᑯᑦᑎᐊᓃᑉᐹ?**
Sukuttianiippa?
Where exactly is it?

ᐅᕝᕙᐅᓇ. <<
Uvvauna.
It's right here.

ᑕᐃᑲ.
Taika.
There it is.

ᐅᒥᐊᑉ ᐊᑖᓃᑦᑐᖅ.
Umiap ataaniittuq.
It is under the boat.

ᐃᓪᓗᑉ ᓴᓂᐊᓃᑦᑐᖅ.
Illuup sanianiittuq.
It is beside the house.

ᐃᓪᓗᑉ ᓯᕐᓗᐊᓪᓗ
ᐊᑯᓐᓂᖓᓃᑦᑐᖅ.
Illuup sirluallu
akunninganiittuq.
It's between the house and
the shed.

photo: Leena Evic

ᖃᐅᒪᐅᓂᖅ

time

ᒫᓐᓇ	maanna	*now*
ᒫᓐᓇᕈᓗᒃ	maannaruluk	*in a little while*
ᐅᓪᓛᖅ	ullaaq	*morning*
ᖁᓛᓂ	qulaani	*noon*
ᐅᓐᓅᒃᓴᖅ (ᐅᓐᓄᓴ)	unnuksaq (unnusa)	*afternoon*
ᐅᓐᓄᒃ	unnuk	*evening*
ᐅᓐᓄᐊᖅ	unnuaq	*night*
ᐅᓪᓗᒥ	ullumi	*today*
ᖃᐅᑉᐸᑦ	qauppat	*tomorrow*
ᐅᖓᓕᐊᒍ	ungaliagu	*the day after tomorrow*
ᐃᑉᐸᔅᓴᖅ	ippassaq	*yesterday*
ᐃᑉᐸᔅᓵᓂ	ippassaani	*the day before yesterday*
ᐅᓪᓗᖅ	ulluq	*day*
ᐅᓪᓗᓕᒫᖅ	ullulimaaq	*all day*
ᖃᐅᑕᒫᑦ	qautamaat	*every day*
ᐱᓇᓲᐊᕈᓯᖅ	pinasuarusiq	*week*
ᐱᓇᓲᐊᕈᓯᐅᑉ ᓄᙳᐊᓂ	pinasuarusiup nunnguani	*on the weekend*
ᐱᓇᓲᐊᕈᓯᐅᓛᖅᑐᖅ	pinasuarusiulaaqtuq	*next week*
ᐱᓇᓲᐊᕈᓯᐅᓚᐅᖅᑐᖅ	pinasuarusiulauqtuq	*last week*
ᐱᓇᓲᐊᕈᓯᖅᑕᒫᑦ	pinasuarusiqtamaat	*weekly*

ᑕᖅᑭᖅ	taqqiq	*month*
ᑕᖅᑭᐅᓛᖅᑐᖅ	taqqiulaaqtuq	*next month*
ᑕᖅᑭᐅᓚᐅᖅᑐᖅ	taqqiulauqtuq	*last month*
ᐊᕐᕋᒎ	arraagu	*year; next year*
ᐊᕐᕋᓂ	arraani	*last year*

MONTHS & SEASONS

Many of the terms used in Inuktitut for telling time were borrowed from English. The modern terms used for the seasons also reflect the European division of the year into four seasons.

The traditional Inuit calendar was much more complex with many seasons named after the activities that took place with the changing weather. For this reason, the Inuit calendar varied from place to place depending on the local climate.

Likewise, the modern words for seasons will be used at different times in different communities due to variations in climate.

Even the names for the days of the week are different, depending on the community you're in. The ones that appear here are based upon the name formats adopted for the Inuktitut "locale" currently found in Microsoft products.

ᔭᓐᓄᐊᕆ	jaannuari	*January*
ᕖᕝᕚᕆ	viivvuari	*February*
ᒫᑦᓯ	maatsi	*March*
ᐃᐳᕆ	iipuri	*April*
ᒪᐃ	mai	*May*
ᔫᓂ	juuni	*June*
ᔪᓚᐃ	julai	*July*
ᐊᒡᒌᓯ	aaggiisi	*August*
ᓯᑎᐱᕆ	sitipiri	*September*
ᐅᑐᐱᕆ	utupiri	*October*
ᓄᕕᐱᕆ	nuvipiri	*November*
ᑎᓯᐱᕆ	tisipiri	*December*

ᐅᑭᐅᖅ	ukiuq	*winter*
ᐅᐱᕐᖓᖅ	upirngaaq	*spring*
ᐊᐅᔭᖅ	aujaq	*summer*
ᐅᑭᐊᔅᓵᖅ	ukiassaaq	*early autumn*
ᐅᑭᐊᖅ	ukiaq	*autumn*

days of the week

ᓈᑦᑏᖑᔭ	naattiinguja	*Sunday*
ᓇᒡᒐᔾᔭᐅ	naggajjau	*Monday*
ᐊᐃᑉᐱᖅ	aippiq	*Tuesday*
ᐱᖓᑦᓯᖅ	pingatsiq	*Wednesday*
ᓯᑕᒻᒥᖅ	sitammiq	*Thursday*
ᑕᓪᓕᕐᒥᖅ	tallirmiq	*Friday*
ᓯᕙᑖᕐᕕᒃ	sivataarvik	*Saturday*

in conversation: **telling time**

>> ᖃᑦᓕᒨᖅᐸ?
qattimuuqpa?
What time is it?

ᐅᐊᒨᖅᑐᖅ. <<
Uamuuqtuq.
It's 1 o'clock.

ᐅᐊᒦᓐᖓᓕᖅᑐᖅ.
Uamiinngaaliqtuq.
*from just after 1:00 to
1:30*

ᑑᒨᓕᖅᑐᖅ.
Tuumuuliqtuq.
*from just after 1:30 to
just before 2:00*

ᑑᒨᖅᑐᖅ.
Tuumuuqtuq.
It's 2 o'clock.

ᑑᒦᓐᖓᓕᖅᑐᖅ.
Tuumiinngaaliqtuq.
from just after 2:00 to 2:30

ᑕᓖᒨᓕᖅᑐᖅ.
Taliimuuliqtuq.
*from just after 2:30 to
just before 3:00*

>> ᖃᑦᓕᒨᖅᐸᑦ?
Qattimuuqpat?
*at what time? (in the
future)*

ᑎᑭᓛᖅᑐᖓ ᐋᑐᕚᒧᑦ <<
ᓇᐃᒨᖅᐸᑦ.
Tikilaaqtunga
Aatuvaamut naimuuqpat.
*I will get to Ottawa at
nine.*

ᐸᐃᒨᖅᑲᑦ ᓂᕆᓂᐊᖅᑐᒍᑦ.
Paimuuqqat
niriniaqtugut.
We will eat at five.

ᐃᓄᐃᑦ
people

family
feelings & opinions
the human body
clothes

photo: Leena Evic

ᐃᓚᒌᑦ
family

FAMILY TERMINOLOGY

Inuktitut has precise vocabulary for describing family relationships. In the case of siblings, different terms are used for older siblings and younger siblings of the same sex and of the opposite sex.

Inuktitut speakers will often address each other directly with these terms, unlike English speakers who tend to use a relative's first name. Don't be surprised to hear brothers and sisters in the same family all addressing each other with different names.

ᐃᓚᒌᑦ	ilagiit	*family*
ᐃᓚᒃᑲ	ilakka	*my family*
ᐊᓈᓇ	anaana	*mother*
ᐊᑖᑕ	ataata	*father*
ᓄᓕᐊᖅ	nuliaq	*wife*
ᐅᐃᒃ	uik	*husband*
ᐊᐃᑉᐸᖅ	aippaq	*partner; common-law*
ᕿᑐᕐᖓᖅ	qiturngaq	*one's own children*
ᐃᕐᓂᖅ	irniq	*son*
ᐸᓂᒃ	panik	*daughter*
ᖃᑕᙳᑏ	qatannguti	*sibling*
ᐊᖏᔪᒃ	angijuk	*older sibling (of same sex)*
ᓄᑲᖅ	nukaq	*younger sibling (of same sex)*
ᐊᓂᒃ	anik	*brother of a female*
ᓇᔭᒃ	najak	*sister of a male*
ᐊᓈᓇᑦᓯᐊᖅ; ᓂᖕᒋᐅᖅ	anaanatsiaq; ningiuq	*grandmother*
ᐊᑖᑦᑦᓯᐊᖅ; ᐃᑦᑐᖅ	ataatatsiaq; ittuq	*grandfather*
ᐃᕐᖑᑕᖅ	irngutaq	*grandchild*

ᕿᑐᕐᖓᖃᖅᐱᑦ?
Qiturngaqaqpit?
Do you have any children?

ᖃᑦᓯᓂᒃ ᕿᑐᕐᖓᖃᖅᐱᑦ?
Qatsinik qiturngaqaqpit?
How many children do you have?

ᐊᑕᐅᓯᕐᒥᒃ ᐃᕐᓂᖃᖅᑐᖓ.
Atausirmik irniqaqtunga.
I have one son.

ᒪᕐᕉᓐᓂᒃ ᐸᓂᖃᖅᑐᖓ.
Marruunnik paniqaqtunga.
I have two daughters.

ᖃᑦᓯᓂᒃ ᖃᑕᙳᑎᖃᖅᐱᑦ?
Qatsinik qatanngutiqaqpit?
How many siblings do you have?

ᐱᖓᓱᓂᒃ ᖃᑕᙳᑎᖃᖅᑐᖓ.
Pingasunik qatanngutiqaqtunga.
I have three siblings.

ᓯᑕᒪᓂᒃ ᖃᑕᙳᑎᖃᖅᑐᖓ.
Sitamanik qatanngutiqaqtunga.
I have four siblings.

ᒪᕐᕈᓕᐊᒥᓂᐅᖃᑎᖃᖅᑐᖓ
marruliaminiuqatiqaqtunga
I have a twin.

ᐊᖏᔪᑦᑎᖅᐹᖑᕖᑦ?
angijuttiqpaanguviit
Are you the oldest?

ᑭᓇ ᐊᖏᔪᑦᑎᖅᐹᖑᕙ?
Kina angijuttiqpaanguva?
Who's the oldest?

ᑭᓇ ᓄᑲᖅᑎᖅᐹᖑᕙ?
Kina nukaqtiqpaanguva?
Who's the youngest?

ᖃᖓᒃᑯᑦ ᓇᓪᓕᐅᑎᓲᖑᕕᑦ?
Qangakkut nalliutisuunguvit?
When is your birthday?

ᑎᒍᐊᖑᕖᑦ?
tiguanguviit?
Were you adopted?

ᑎᒍᐊᖑᔪᖓ.
tiguangujunga
I am adopted.

ᑭᓇᒥᒃ ᐊᑖᑕᖃᖅᐱᑦ?
Kinamik ataataqaqpit?
Who is your father?

ᐊᑖᑕᖃᖅᑐᖓ ...ᒥᒃ
ataataqaqtunga ...mik
My father is...(person's name)

ᑭᓇᒥᒃ ᐋᓈᓇᖃᖅᐱᑦ?
Kinamik anaanaqaqpit?
Who is your mother?

ᐋᓈᓇᖃᖅᑐᖓ ...ᒥᒃ
anaanaqaqtunga ...mik
My mother is... (person's name)

ᑲᑎᑎᑕᐅᓯᒪᕕᑦ
katititausimavit
Are you married?

ᑭᓇᒥᒃ ᐅᐃᖃᖅᐱᑦ?
Kinamik uiqaqpit?
Who is your husband?

ᑭᓇᒥᒃ ᓄᓕᐊᖃᖅᐱᑦ?
Kinamik nuliaqaqpit?
Who is your wife?

people : family

ᐃᓯᐱᓂᐊᓂᖅ ᐊᒻᒪ
ᐅᖅᑐᓐᖅᐊᓯᓂᖅ ᐃᓯᒪᒋᔭᒥᒃ
feelings & opinions

ᖁᕕᐊᓱᐳᑉᐱᑦ?	quviasuppiit?	*Are you happy?*
ᐄ, ᖁᕕᐊᓱᒃᑐᖓ	ii, quviasuktunga	*Yes, I am happy.*
ᐅᒃᒍᐊᖅᓯᒪᔪᖓ	ugguaqsimajunga	*I am regretful*
ᐅᒃᒍᐊᕐᓇᐅᒐᓗᐊᖅ	ugguarnaugaluaq	*Sorry to hear it.*
ᓂᖕᖓᐅᒪᔪᖓ	ninngaumajunga	*I am angry.*
ᑲᖕᖒᓱᑦᑐᖓ	kanngusuttunga	*I am feeling shy.*
ᖁᓱᔪᖓ	qusujunga	*I am sad. (S. Baffin)*
ᓄᒫᒋᔭᖓ	numaagijanga	*It makes him sad.*
		(N. Baffin)
ᑲᖕᖒᓱᒃᑐᑎᑦ	kanngusuktutit	*You are feeling shy.*
ᑲᖕᖒᒋᔭᐃᑦ	kanngugijait	*He makes you feel shy.*
ᑲᑉᐱᐊᓱᒃᑐᖓ	kappiasuktunga	*I am afraid.*
ᑲᑉᐱᐊᒋᔭᖓ	kappiagijanga	*He is scared of her.*
ᐃᖅᐊᖕᖒᖅᑐᖓ	iqiannguqtunga	*I am tired of doing*
		something.
ᑲᔾᔮᓇᖅᑐᖅ	kajjaanaqtuq	*pleasant time or place*
ᑐᓴᕐᓂᕆᔭᕋ	tusarnirijara	*I like the sound of it.*
ᑐᓴᕆᐊᖓ ᖁᕕᐊᓇᖅᑐᖅ.	Tusarianga quvianaqtuq.	*Happy to hear it.*
ᐊᓱᑯᓗᒃ	asukuluk	*That's very good to hear.*
ᖃᐊᖅᑲᐅᔪᖓ	qiaqqaujunga	*I was crying.*
ᐅᑎᕈᒪᔪᖓ	utirumajunga	*I want to go back.*
ᐱᔭᕇᖅᑐᖓ	pijariiqtunga	*I'm done.*
ᐃᓯᒪᔪᓐᓇᐃᓕᑦᑎᐊᖅᑐᖓ	isumajunnailittiaqtunga	*I can't think anymore.*
ᐃᖅᑲᐅᒪᕕᐃᑦ?	iqqaumaviit?	*Do you remember?*
ᐳᐃᒍᕋᖅᖃᐅᖕᒋᑦᑐᖅ	puigurassaungittuq	*It's hard to forget.*
ᐃᖅᑲᐅᒪᖕᖏᑦᑐᖓ	iqqaumanngittunga	*I don't remember.*

ᖃᓄᕐᖠ ᐃᓱᒪᒋᕕᐅᒃ?
Qanurli isumagiviuk?
What do you think of him/her?

ᐃᓄᑦᑎᐊᕚᓘᒃ
inuttiavaaluk
He/she is a good person.

ᐅᖅᐸᕋᔪᐃᑦᑐᖅ; ᓂᓪᓕᕋᔪᐃᑦᑐᖅ
uqarajuittuq; nillirajuittuq
He/she is very quiet.

ᐃᓅᖃᓐᓂᖅᑐᐊᓗᒃ
inuuqanniqtualuk
She is easy to get along with.

ᓂᙵᓴᕋᐃᑦᑐᖅ
ninngassaraittuq
He/she has a quick temper.

ᖃᓄᐃᒋᕕᐅᒃ?
qanuigiviuk?
How do you feel about him/her?

ᐊᑲᐅᒋᔭᕋ
akaugijara
I like her / him.

ᐊᑲᐅᒋᖕᒋᑕᕋ/ᓈᒻᒪᒋᖕᒋᑕᕋ
akaugingitara /naammagingitara
I'm not happy with her / him.

ᓇᓪᓕᒋᔭᕋ
nalligijara
I love her / him.

ᓇᓪᓕᒋᕙᒋᑦ
nalligivagit
I love you.

ᐅᖓᓕᖅᑕᒋᑦ
ungaliqtagit
I miss you.

ᐃᓕᕋᒋᔭᕋ.
iliragijara
I'm afraid to disappoint him/her.

ᖃᓄᕐᖠ ᐃᓱᒪᕕᑦ?
Qanurli isumavit?
What do you think? (to 1 person)

ᖃᓄᕐᖠ ᐃᓱᒪᕕᓯᒃ?
Qanurli isumavisik?
What do you think? (to 2 people)

ᖃᓄᕐᖠ ᐃᓱᒪᕕᓯ?
Qanurli isumavisi?
And what do you think? (3+people)

ᐱᐅᒋᔭᕋ
piugijara
I like it.

ᖁᕕᐊᒋᔭᕋ
quviagijara
I enjoy it.

ᐊᓕᐊᓇᐃᑦ; ᖁᕕᐊᓇᓪᓚᕆᑦᑐᖅ
alianait; quvianallarittuq
It's wonderful.

ᖁᕕᐊᒋᖕᒋᑕᕋ
quviaginngittara
I don't like it.

ᑲᒪᓇᖅᑐᖅ; ᐅᑉᐱᕐᓇᖕᒋᑦᑐᖅ
kamanaqtuq/uppirnangittuq
It's amazing; unbelievable.

ᖁᕕᐊᓇᖕᒡᓕᕆᑦᑐᖅ
quviananngillarittuq
It's terrible.

ᖃᐱᓚᒋᔭᕋ
qapilagijara
I find it dreary.

ᑕᒥ

the human body

ᓴᐅᒥᒃ	saumik	*left*
ᑕᓕᖅᐱᒃ	taliqpik	*right*
ᑕᒥ	timi	*body*
ᐅᕕᓂᒃ	uvinik	*skin*
ᓂᐊᖁᖅ	niaquq	*head*
ᓄᔭᑦ	nujat	*hair*
ᓄᔭᑭᑦᑐᖅ	nujakittuq	*short hair*
ᓄᔭᑯᑖᒃ	nujakutaak	*long hair*
ᐃᕿᓱᓕᒃ	iqisulik	*curly hair*
ᓄᔭᖕᒋᑦ ᖃᕐᓂᖅᑐᑦ	nujangit qirniqtut	*dark hair*
ᓄᔭᖕᒋᑦ ᖁᕐᔪᑦ	nujangit qurjut	*light hair*
ᕿᐃᖅ	qiiq	*white hair*
ᐅᒥᓕᒃ	umilik	*a person with a beard*
ᑲᔾᔨᖅ	kajjiq	*top of the head*
ᐃᖅᓴᖅ	iqsaq	*cheek (by the nose)*
ᐅᓗᐊᒃ	uluak	*cheek (toward the ear)*
ᓯᐅᑦ	siut	*ear*
ᑭᓇᖅ	kiinaq	*face*
ᕿᙵᖅ	qinnguq	*brow*
ᖃᐅᖅ	qauq	*forehead*
ᖃᓪᓗ	qallu	*eyebrow*
ᕿᒥᕆᐊᑦ	qimiriat	*eyelashes*
ᐃᔨ	iji	*eye*
ᕿᖕᒐᖅ	qingaq	*nose*
ᖃᖅᑐ	qaqtu	*lower lip*
ᖃᓂᖅ	qaniq	*mouth*
ᑭᒍᑎ	kiguti	*tooth*

ᐅᖃᖅ	uqaq	*tongue*
ᖁᖓᓯᖅ	qungasiq	*neck*
ᑐᓄᓱᒃ	tunusuk	*nape of the neck*
ᑐᓄ	tunu	*back*
ᕿᒥᕐᓗᒃ	qimirluk	*spine*
ᓴᓂᕋᖅ	saniraq	*side (of body)*
ᑐᐃ	tui	*shoulder*
ᑕᓕᖅ	taliq	*arm*
ᐃᑯᓯᒃ	ikusik	*elbow*
ᐊᒡᒐᐅᑦ	aggaut	*forearm*
ᐸᕝᕕᒃ	pavvik	*wrist*
ᐊᒡᒐᒃ	aggak	*hand*
ᐃᑎᒪᒃ	itimak	*palm of the hand*
ᑯᑦᓗ	kullu	*thumb*
ᑎᑭᖅ	tikiq	*index finger*
ᓴᕝᕕᒃ	savvik	*chest*
ᐃᕕᐊᖐᒃ	iviangiik	*breasts*
ᓈᖅ	naaq	*stomach*
ᖃᓚᓯᖅ	qalasiq	*belly button*
ᕿᑎᖅ	qitiq	*waist*
ᐅᑉᐸᑏᒃ	uppatiik	*hips*
ᐅᑦᓲᒃ	utsuuk	*vagina*
ᐅᓱᒃ	usuk	*penis*
ᓄᓗ	nulu	*buttock*
ᓂᐅ	niu	*leg*
ᖁᑦᑐᕋᖅ	qutturaq	*thigh*
ᓰᖅᑯᖅ	siiqquq	*knee*
ᑲᓈᒃ	kanaak	*shin*
ᓯᖏᕐᓂᖅ	singirniq	*ankle*
ᐃᓯᒐᒃ	isigak	*foot*
ᑭᒻᒥᒃ	kimmik	*heel*
ᐳᑐᒍᖅ	putuguq	*toe*

ᕿᐅᕕᑦ?
qiuvit?
Are you cold?

ᕿᐅᔪᖓ
qiujunga
I am cold.

ᐅᖅᑯᔪᖓ
uqquujunga
I'm hot.

ᑭᐊᑦᑐᖓ
kiattunga
I am sweating.

ᐅᐃᕐᖓᖅᑐᖓ
uirngaqtunga
I'm sleepy.

ᐊᑲᐅᑦᓯᐊᙱᑦᑐᖓ
akautsianngittunga
I don't feel well.

ᓂᐊᖁᓐᖑᔪᖓ
niaqunngujunga
I have a headache.

ᖃᓂᒪᔪᖓ
qanimajunga
I am sick.

ᖁᐃᖅᓱᖅᑐᖓ
quiqsuqtunga
I am coughing.

ᓄᕙᑦᑐᖓ.
nuvattunga
I have a cold.

ᐆᑎᕐᓈᖅᑐᖓ
uutirnaqtunga
I have a fever.

ᓈᖕᖑᔪᖓ
naanngujunga
I have a stomach ache.

ᒥᕆᐊᖕᖑᔪᖓ
mirianngujunga
I feel nauseous.

ᒥᕆᐊᖅᑲᐅᔪᖓ
miriaqqaujunga
I threw up.

ᕿᑎᕐᓗᑦᑐᖓ
qitirluttunga
I have a sore back.

ᑐᓄᒥᒍᑦ ᐋᓐᓂᖅᑐᒥᓂᐅᒻᒪᑦ.
Tunumigut aanniqtuminiummat.
He hurt his back.

ᒪᑦᑐᑎᖅᓵᖃᖅᐱᑦ?
mattutissaqaqpit?
Do you have a band-aid?

ᐊᐅᓈᖅᑐᖓ.
aunaaqtunga
I am bleeding.

ᑐᓯᐊᑦᑐᖓ
tusiattunga
I am limping.

ᐋᓐᓂᐊᕕᒃ ᓱᑰᑦᑎᐊᓃᑉᐸ?
Aanniavik sukuttianiippa?
Where is the nursing station / hospital ?

ᓱᓪᓗᓂ ᐋᓐᓂᕐᓂᖅᐸ?
Sulluni aannirniqpa?
What was he doing that he hurt himself?

in conversation: **where does it hurt?**

» ᐋᓐᓂᐊᕖᑦ?
aanniaviit?
Are you in pain?

ᒪᐃᑦᑐᖅ «
maittuq
It hurts.

» ᓇᐅᒃᑯᑦ?
naukkut?
Where?

ᒪᐅᓇ «
mauna
Around here

ᑕᒪᐅᓇ
tamauna
Right here.

ᓂᐊᖁᒃᑯᑦ
niaqukkut
My head.

ᑕᓕᒃᑯᑦ
talikkut
My arm.

» ᐊᐅᓈᖅᑐᑎᑦ
aunaaqtutit
You are bleeding.

ᐊᐅᓈᖅᑯᖓ? «
aunaaqqunga?
Am I bleeding?

ᑭᓕᖅᑐᖓ «
kiliqtunga
I cut myself.

ᐃᒻᒪᑦᑐᖅ
immattuq
It is infected.

ᕿᕿᓯᒪᔪᑎᑦ
qiqisimajutit
You have frostbite.

ᕿᕿᑉᐸᓪᓚᐃᔪᒥᓂᐅᔪᖓ.
qiqippallaijuminiujunga.
I think I have frostbite.

ᐊᓐᓄᕌᑦ
clothing

IN CONTEXT

Traditionally-made clothing is widely used throughout Nunavut. Kamiik, mitts and some parkas and snow pants are still made with seal, caribou and bear skins. Skin clothing is much better at keeping the wearer warm and dry than manufactured clothing. Nonetheless, southern fabrics are used by many sewers, especially for the amautit worn by mothers in most communities.

ᐊᓐᓄᕌᑦ	annuraat	*clothing*
ᐊᒡᒑᒃ	aggaak	*gloves*
ᐊᒪᐅᑎ	amauti	*parka with pouch at the back for carrying a child*
ᐊᑯᖅ	akuq	*long-tailed amauti*
ᐊᖕᒋᔪᖅᑕᐅᔭᖅ	angijuqtaujaq	*skirted style amauti*
ᖃᑦᓱᖕᒐᐅᑦ	qatsungaut	*tie for the amauti*
ᖁᓕᑦᑕᐅᔭᖅ	qulittaujaq	*parka (contemporary)*
ᖁᓕᑦᑕᖅ	qulittaq	*caribou parka with fur outside*
ᐊᑎᒋ	atigi	*traditional caribou parka with fur inside*
ᓯᓚᐹᖅ	silapaaq	*parka outer shell*
ᔭᐃᑲᒃ	jaikak	*jacket*
ᖃᕐᓕᐊᓘᒃ	qarlialuuk	*wind pants*
ᐊᖕᒋᔪᖅᑕᖅ	angijuqtaq	*skirt*

ᐊᑕᔪᖅ	atajuq	*dress*
ᔭᐃᑲᒃᑕᕇᒃ	jaikaktariik	*suit*
ᐃᑭᐊᖅᑎᖅ	ikiaqtiq	*shirt*
ᑭᐊᑎ	kiati	*blouse*
ᐅᐊᓯᑯᐊᖅ	uasikuaq	*vest*
ᐅᕕᓂᕈᖅ	uviniruq	*t-shirt*
ᓄᐃᔭᒐᖅ; ᖃᓕᐹᖅ	nuijagaq; qalipaaq	*sweater*
ᖃᕐᓖᒃ	qarliik	*pants*
ᐃᑉᐱᐊᕐᔪᒃ	ippiarjuk	*pocket*
ᕿᓗᐊᖅ	qiluaq	*belt*
ᐃᓯᒐᐅᔮᒃ	isigaujaak	*shoes*
ᑲᒫᓘᒃ	kamaaluuk	*rubber boots*
ᑲᒫᓘᒃ ᐅᑭᐅᖅᓯᐅᑏᒃ	kamaaluuk ukiuqsiutiik	*winter boots*
ᑲᒦᒃ	kamiik	*skin boots*
ᑲᒥᑯᑖᒃ	kamikutaak	*long boots*
ᓇᓴᖅ	nasaq	*hat*
ᐳᐊᓘᒃ	pualuuk	*mittens*
ᖁᖓᓯᕈᖅ	qungasiruq	*scarf; men's tie*
ᓇᒻᒪᒑᖅ	nammagaaq	*knapsack*
ᐴᖅ	puuq	*bag; sack*
ᓯᕿᖅ	siqiiq	*zipper*
ᐃᓯᕆᐅᑦ	isiriut	*button*
ᓇᕿᑦᑕᖅᑐᖅ	naqittaqtuq	*snaps*
ᓯᐅᒻᒥᐅᑖᒃ	siummiutaak	*earrings*
ᑕᓕᐊᖅ	taliaq	*wrist watch; bracelet*
ᓇᒡᒍᐊᕐᒥᒃ; ᐊᒡᒐᒻᒥᒃ	nagguarmik; aggammik	*ring*
ᐅᔭᒥᒃ	ujamik	*necklace*
ᑎᖅᑭᐊᓕᒃ	tiqqialik	*baseball cap*
ᐃᒡᓗᒌᒃ	iglugiik	*pair*
ᐃᒡᓗᐃᓐᓇᖅ	igluinnaq	*one of a pair*
ᐃᒡᓗᐊ	iglua	*the other one of a pair; the matching one*

people : clothing

ᒥᑭᓗᐊᖅᑐᖅ
mikiluaqtuq
It is too small.

ᐊᖏᓗᐊᖅᑐᖅ
angiluaqtuq
It is too big.

ᓈᒻᒪᒋᕕᐅᒃ?
naammagiviuk?
Does it fit; Is it O.K.?

ᓈᒻᒪᑦᑐᖅ
naammattuq
It fits; it's O.K.

ᓈᒻᒪᑦᑎᐊᖅᑐᖅ
naammattiaqtuq
It fits perfectly.

ᔭᐃᑲᒐ ᒥᑭᒋᓕᖅᑕᕋ.
Jaikaga mikigiliqtara?
My jacket is too small for me.

ᐱᐅᒋᔭᕋ ᐊᑐᖅᑕᐃᑦ.
piugijara atuqtait.
I like the one your wearing.

ᐱᐅᒋᔭᕋ ᐊᒥᐊᖓ.
Piugijara amianga.
I like the colour.

ᐱᐅᒋᙱᑦᑕᕋ ᐊᒥᐊᖓ.
Piuginngittara amianga.
I don't like the colour.

ᑭᓱᒥᑦ ᓴᓇᓯᒪᒻᒪᑦ?
Kisumit sanasimammat?
What's it made out of?

ᐅᓇ ᑭᐊᑉ ᒥᖅᓱᕐᓂᕐᒪᒍ?
Una kiap miqsurnirmagu?
Who sewed this?

ᐃᓯᒑᐅᔭᖅᑖᕆᐊᖃᖅᑐᖓ
isigaujaqtaariaqaqtunga
I need to get shoes.

ᓇᑭᓪᓕ ᓂᐅᕕᐊᕆᓐᓂᕋᕕᐅᒃ?
Nakilli niuviarinniraviuk?
Where did you buy it?

ᐅᖅᑰᔾᔫᒥᔪᓂᒃ ᐊᓐᓄᕌᖅᓯᒪᓂᐊᖅᑯᑎᑦ ᐅᓪᓗᒥ.
Uqquujjuumijunik annuraaqsimaniaqqutit ullumi.
Wear warm clothes today.

ᔭᐃᑲᐃᑦ ᓯᕿᕐᓗᒍ.
Jaikait siqiirlugu.
Please zip up your jacket.

ᑲᒥᓪᓚᕐᓗᑎᑦ
kamillarlutit
Please take your boots off.

ᑲᒥᓪᓚᖏᓪᓗᑎᑦ
kamillangillutit
Please don't take your boots off.

ᐊᒡᒑᒃ ᐃᓪᓗᒌᒃ
aggaak illugiik
a pair of gloves

ᐊᒡᒑᖅ ᐃᓪᓗᐃᓐᓇᖅ
aggaaq illuinnaq
a single glove

ᐊᒡᒑᒃ ᐃᓪᓗᒌᙱᑦᑑᒃ
aggaak illugiinngittuuk
two gloves that don't match

in conversation: who does this belong to?

>> ᑭᐊᑉ ᐅᓇ?
Kiap una?
Who does this belong to? <<

>> ᐱᑦ?
piit?
Is it your's?

ᐱᒐ
piga <<
It's mine.

ᐅᓇ ᐱᖓ.
Una pinga.
It's his/hers.

ᐅᓇ ᐱᖓᑦ.
Una pingat.
It's theirs.

>> ᐅᓇ ᑭᐊᑉ ᔭᐃᒃᖓ?
Una kiap jaikanga?
Who does this jacket belong to?

ᐅᕙᖓ, ᔭᐃᑲᒐ.
Uvanga, jaikaga. <<
That's my jacket.

>> ᐅᑯᐊᒃ ᑭᐊᑉ ᐳᐊᓗᖕᒃ?
Ukuak kiap pualungik?
Who do these mitts belong to?

ᑖᒃᑯᐊᒃ ᔨᓛᐅᑉ ᐳᐊᓗᖕᒃ.
Taakkuak Jiilaup pualungik. <<
These are Jiila's mitts.

>> ᐅᓇ ᐊᑐᕐᓚᒍ
Una aturlagu?
Can I use (borrow) this?

ᐊᑐᕐᓇᖅᑕᐃᑦ.
Aturunnaqtait. <<
You can use this.

>> ᑕᑯᔭᐅᓚᐅᖅᑉ ᐳᐊᓗᒪ ᐃᓪᓗᐊ?
Takujaulauqpa pualuma illua?
Have you seen my other mitt?

ᐃᑦᓯᕙᐅᑕᐅᑉ ᐊᑖᓃᑉᐸᓪᓚᐃᔪᖅ
Itsivautaup ataaniippallaijuq.
It's probably underneath the chair.

people : clothing

45

ᐃᓅᖅᑲᑎᒌᓐᓂᖅ
social

photo: Nunavut Tourism

greetings
making plans
a night on the town

ᑐᙵᓵᕆᔾᔪᑎᑦ

greetings

ᐅᓪᓛᒃᑯᑦ
ullaakkut
Good Morning

ᐅᓐᓄᓴᒃᑯᑦ
unnusakkut
Good Afternoon

ᐅᓪᓗᒃᑯᑦ
ullukkut
Good Day (afternoon)

ᐅᓐᓄᒃᑯᑦ
unnukkut
Good Evening

ᐅᓐᓄᖅᑲᑦᑎᐊᕆᑦ
unnuqattiarit
Good Night; Have a good evening.

ᑐᙵᓱᒋᑦ
tunngasugit
welcome (speaking to 1 person)

ᑐᙵᓱᒋᑦᓯᒃ
tunngasugitsik
welcome (speaking to 2 people)

ᑐᙵᓱᒋᑦᓯ
tunngasugitsi
welcome (speaking to 3 or more)

ᐅᐊᑦᑎᐊᕈᑦᑕᐅᖅ
uattiaruttauq
See you in a little while.

ᑕᑯᓛᕆᕗᒍᒃ
takulaarivuguk
See you again. (to 1 person).

ᑕᑯᓛᕆᕗᒍᑦ
takulaarivugut
See you again. (to 2 + people).

ᐅᓪᓗᖅᑲᑦᓯᐊᕆᑦ
ulluqatsiarit
Have a good day (speaking to 1).

ᐅᓪᓗᖅᑲᑦᓯᐊᕆᑦᓯᒃ
ulluqatsiaritsik
Have a good day (speaking to 2).

ᐅᓪᓗᖅᑲᑦᓯᐊᕆᑦᓯ
ulluqatsiaritsi
Have a good day (speaking to 3+).

ᑕᕝᕙᐅᕗᑎᑦ
tavvauvutit
Good-bye (speaking to 1)

ᑕᕝᕙᐅᕗᓯᒃ
tavvauvusik
Good-bye (speaking to 2)

ᑕᕝᕙᐅᕗᓯ
tavvauvusi
Good-bye (speaking to 3+)

ᖃᑯᒍᑦᑕᐅᖅ
qakuguttauq
until next time

in conversation: **how are you?**

» ᖃᓄᐃᑉᐱᑦ?
Qanuippit?
How are you?

ᖃᓄᐃᙱᑦᑐᖓ.
Qanuinngittunga.
I'm fine. «

ᐊᑲᐅᑦᓯᐊᙱᑦᑐᖓ.
Akautsianngittunga.
I don't feel very well.

ᓄᕙᑦᑐᖓ.
nuvattunga
I have a cold.

» ᐅᐃᕐᖓᖅᐱᑦ?
Uirngaqpit?
Are you sleepy?

ᐅᐃᕐᖓᖅᑐᖓ.
Uirngaqtunga.
I am sleepy.

» ᓯᓂᑦᑎᐊᖅᑲᐅᕕᑦ?
Sinittiaqqauvit?
Did you sleep well?

ᐄ, ᓯᓂᑦᑎᐊᖅᑲᐅᔪᖓ.
ii, sinittiaqqaujunga.
Yes, I slept well. «

ᐋᒡᒐᐃ,
ᓯᓂᑦᑎᐊᖅᑲᐅᙱᑦᑐᖓ.
Aaggai,
sinittiaqqaunngittunga.
No, I didn't sleep well.

» ᖃᓄᐃᑉᐱᓯᒃ?
Qanuippisik?
How are the two of you?

ᖃᓄᐃᙱᑦᑐᒃ.
Qanuinngittuguk.
We are fine (the two of us). «

» ᖃᓄᐃᑉᐱᓯ?
Qanuippisi?
How are all of you?

ᖃᓄᐃᙱᑦᑐᒍᑦ.
Qanuinngittugut.
We're fine (3+). «

» ᖃᓄᐃᑉᐸ?
Qanuippa?
How is he/she?

ᖃᓄᐃᙱᑦᑐᖅ
Qanuinngittuq.
She / he is fine. «

ᓱᕙᒪᓂᖅ

making plans

ᓱᕕᑦ?	suvit?	*What are you doing?*
ᓱᓂᐊᖅᐱᑦ?	suniaqpit?	*What will you be doing later?*
ᓱᓛᖅᐱᑦ?	sulaaqpit?	*What will you be doing (tomorrow or later)?*
ᖃᖓ?	qanga?	*when?*
ᒫᓐᓇ	maanna	*now*
ᒫᓐᓇᕈᓗᒃ	maannaruluk	*soon*
ᐅᐊᑦᑎᐊᕈ	uattiaru	*later*
ᐅᐊᑦᑎᐊᕈᒃᑲᓐᓂᖅ	uattiarukkanniq	*in a little while*
ᐅᓪᓗᒥ	ullumi	*today*
ᖃᐅᐸᑦ	qauppat	*tomorrow*
ᐱᓇᓱᐊᕈᓯᐅᑉ ᓄᙳᐊᓂ	pinasuarusiup nunnguani	*on the weekend*
ᐱᓇᓱᐊᕈᓯᐅᓛᖅᑐᖅ	pinasuarusiulaaqtuq	*next week*
ᖃᑦᑎᒨᖅᑲᑦ?	qattimuuqqat?	*What time?*
ᖃᓄᑎᒋ?	qanutigi?	*for how long?*
ᐄ	ii	*yes*
ᐋᒡᒐ	aagga	*no*
ᒪᒥᐊᓇᖅ	mamianaq	*sorry*
ᐃᒻᒪᖃ	immaqa	*maybe*
ᐄᖃᐃ	iiqai	*possibly*
ᖃᖓ?	qanga?	*when?*
ᐃᖅᑲᓇᐃᔭᕇᕈᒪ	iqqanaijariiruma	*after work*
ᓇᒥ?	nami?	*where?*
ᐅᕙᑦᑎᓐᓂ	uvattinni	*at my place*
ᐃᓕᔅᓯᓐᓂ	ilissinni	*at your place*
ᓂᕆᕕᒻᒥ	nirivimmi	*at the restaurant*

ᐱᓇᓱᐊᕈᓯᐅᓛᖅᑐᒥ ᓱᓛᖅᐱᑦ?
Pinasuarusiulaaqtumi sulaaqpit?
What are you doing next week?

ᖃᐅᑉᐸᓪᓕ?
Qauppalli?
What about tomorrow?

ᐱᓇᓱᐊᕈᓯᐅᓛᖅᑐᒥᓪᓕ?
pinasuarusiulaaqtumilli?
What about next week?

ᓈᒻᒪᑦᑐᖅ
naammattuq
It's O.K.

ᐅᕙᓐᓄᑦ ᐅᓐᓄᓴᒃᑯᑦ ᐱᐅᓂᖅᓴᖅ.
Uvannut unnusakkut piuniqsaq.
For me, the afternoon is better.

ᐸᐃᒨᖅᑲᑦ ᐅᕙᓐᓄᑦ ᐊᑲᐅᓂᖅᓴᖅ
Paimuuqqat uvannut akauniqsaq.
5:00 would be better for me.

ᐅᕙᑎᓐᓄᑦ ᓂᕆᔭᖅᑐᕐᓂᐊᕋᑦᑕ.
Uvatinnut nirijaqturniaratta.
We are going to eat at my place.

ᑕᕐᕆᔭᕐᓂᐊᖅᑐᖓ
tarrijarniaqtunga
I'm going to watch a movie.

ᐸᑎᕆᐊᖅᑐᖓ
paatiriaqtunga
I'm going to a party.

ᐲᑕ ᐸᑎᖅᑎᑦᑎᔪᖅ ᐊᖏᕐᕋᒥᓂ.
Piita paatiqtittijuq angirramini.
Piita is having a party at his house.

ᐱᖃᑕᐅᔪᒪᕕᑦ?
piqataujumaviit?
Do you want to come along?

ᑭᒃᑯᓪᓗ ᑕᐃᑯᙵᓂᐊᖅᐸᑦ?
Kikkullu taikunnganiaqpat?
Who else is going?

ᐅᐸᓚᐅᖅᐸ?
upalauqpa?
Did he show up?

ᐅᐸᓚᐅᖅᑐᖅ
upalauqtuq
She showed up.

ᐅᐸᓚᐅᙱᑦᑐᑦ
upalaunngittut
They didn't show up.

ᐊᐃᓂᐊᖅᑕᕋ
ainiaqtara
I will pick her up later.

ᐊᐃᔭᐅᔪᒪᒍᕕᑦ ᐊᐃᔪᓐᓇᖅᑕᒋᑦ.
Aijaujumaguvit aijunnaqtagit.
I can pick you up if you like.

ᐊᖅᑯᓵᕐᓂᐊᖅᑕᒋᑦ
aqqusaarniaqtagit
I will pick you up along the way.

ᐊᖅᑯᓴᐅᑎᓂᐊᖅᑕᒋᑦ
aqqusautiniaqtagit
I will drop you off along the way.

ᖃᐃᓂᐊᖅᑐᖓ
qainiaqtunga
I'll be there.

ᖃᐃᔾᔮᙱᑦᑐᖓ
qaijjaanngittunga
I won't be coming.

ᖃᐃᓂᐊᖅᐳᑎᑦ
qainiaqputit
Come over later.

>> ᐅᐊᓄᕽ ᓯᓂᐊᖅᐱᑦ?
Unnusa suniaqpit?
*What are you doing this
afternoon?*

ᐊᒡᒌ / ᐊᒪᐃ. <<
Aatsuu / aamai.
I don't know.

ᐅᐊᓄᖅ ᓯᓂᐊᖅᐱᑦ?
Unnuk suniaqpit?
*What are you doing this
evening?*

ᒧᒥᕆᐊᖅᑐᖓ
mumiriaqtunga
I am going dancing.

>> ᖃᐅᐸᑦ ᓯᓛᖅᐱᑦ?
Qauppat sulaaqpit?
*What are you doing
tomorrow?*

ᑐᒃᑐᓕᐊᖅᑐᖓ. <<
Tuttuliaqtunga
*I am going caribou
hunting.*

>> ᐱᓇᓱᕈᓯᐅᑉ ᓄᓐᖑᐊᓂ
ᓯᓂᐊᖅᐱᑦ?
Pinasuarusiup nunnguani
suniaqpit?
*What are you doing this
weekend?*

ᐅᖓᓕᐊᒍ ᖃᒧᑕᐅᔭᓛᖅᑐᖓ. <<
Ungaliagu
qamutaujalaaqtunga.
*The day after tomorrow, I will
be going ski-dooing.*

>> ᑐᓯ!
Tusu!
I'm envious!

ᐃᓚᐅᔪᒪᕕᐃᑦ? <<
ilaujumaviit?
*Do you want to come
along?*

>> ᐃᓚᐅᔪᓐᓇᖅᐳᖓ?
ilaujunnaqpunga?
May I come along?

ᑐᓐᖓᓱᑉᐳᑎᑦ ᐃᓚᐅᔪᒪᒍᕕᑦ. <<
Tunngasupputit
ilaujumaguvit.
*You're welcome to come
along.*

>> ᐅᖃᐊᓚᕕᒋᓐᖓ.
Uqaalaviginnga.
Call me.

ᑕᓖᒦᓐᖓᓕᖅᐸᑦ
ᐅᖃᐊᓚᕕᒋᓛᖅᐸᒋᑦ. <<
Taliimiinngaaliqpat
uqaalavigilaaqpagit.
I will call you after three.

ᓄᓇᓕᖕᓂ ᐅᐸᒐᔅᓴᐃᑦ

a night on the town

ᓂᕆᕕᔾᔪᐊᖅ	nirivijjuaq	*community feast*
ᓇᓪᓕᐅᓂᖅᓯᐅᖅᑐᖅ	nalliuniqsiuqtuq	*having a birthday party*
ᒧᒥᖅᑐᑦ	mumiqtut/suluvittut	*people dancing*
ᐱᖖᒍᐊᖅᑐᑦ	pinnguaqtut	*people playing games*
ᐱᓂᑭᓴᐅᑎᔪᑦ	pinikisautijut	*competitions*
ᓂᔾᔭᐅᓯᔭᖅᑐᑦ	nijjausijaqtut	*playing music*
ᓂᔾᔭᐅᓯᔭᖅᑎᑦ	nijjausijaqtit	*musicians; band*
ᓂᔾᔮᔪᑦ/ᑐᓴᕋᓐᓈᒐᑦ	nijjaajut/tusarannaagat	*music*
ᐃᖖᒋᕈᑦ	inngirut	*accordion*
ᑯᒃᑭᑦᑕᐹᕈᑦ	kukkittapaarut	*guitar*
ᐱᐊᓇ	piana	*piano*
ᐊᓇᐅᓪᓚᒐᑦ	anaullagat	*drums*
ᐃᖖᒋᖅᑎ	inngiqti	*singer*
ᓂᕆᕕᒃ	nirivik	*restaurant*
ᐃᒥᕋᓚᕝᕕᒃ	imiralavvik	*bar*
ᓖᔾᔭ	liijja	*the Legion*
ᑮᓇᐅᔭᖅ	kiinaujaq	*money*
ᑖᑦᓯ	taatsi	*taxi*
ᐱᔨᑲᑖᖅ	pijikataaq	*waiter*
ᐊᑭᓕᔅᓴᖅ	akilissaq	*the bill*
ᓯᒡᒐᓕᐊᑦ	siggaliat	*cigarettes*
ᐃᓐᓇᖅ/ᑲᓱᒃ	innaq/kasuk	*lighter*
ᕙᐃᓂ	vaini	*wine*
ᐱᐊ	pia	*beer*
ᐃᒥᖅ	imiq	*water*
ᑳᐱ	kaapi	*coffee*
ᑏ	tii	*tea*

ᓇᒥ ᐃᑦᓯᕚᕈᒪᕕᑦ?
Nami itsivaarumavit?
Where do you want to sit?

ᓇᒥ ᐃᑦᓯᕚᕐᓂᐊᕋᓐᓄᒃ?
Nami itsivaarniarannuk?
Where are we going to sit?

ᒫᓂ ᐃᑦᓯᕚᖅᑐᖃᖅᐸ?
Maani itsivaaqtuqaqpa?
Is anyone sitting here?

ᑕᒫᓃᑦᑐᖃᙱᑦᑐᖅ
tamaaniittuqanngittuq
There is no one here.

ᐅᓇ ᐃᑦᓯᕙᐅᑕᖅ ᐊᑐᕈᓐᓇᖅᐸᕋ?
Una itsivautaq aturunnaqpara?
May I use this chair?

ᐄ, ᐊᑐᕈᒃ.
ii, aturuk.
Go ahead and use it.

ᐅᓇ ᐃᕿᐊᓇᖅᑐᐊᓗᒃ.
Una iqianaqtualuk.
This is so boring.

ᐅᓇ ᖁᕕᐊᓇᖅᑐᐊᓗᒃ.
Una quvianaqtualuk.
This is lots of fun.

ᑐᓵᕐᓂᕆᓪᓚᕆᑦᑕᒃᑲ ᐃᙱᖅᑐᑦ.
Tusarnirillarittakka inngiqtut.
I really like the band.

ᓂᔾᔭᐅᓯᔭᖅᏘᑦ ᓇᒥᒥᐅᑕᐅᒻᒪᑕ?
Nijjausijaqtiit namimiutaummata?
Where are the band from?

ᑐᓴᓐᓂᕆᙱᑕᕋ ᓂᔾᔮᔪᖅ
Tusanniringitara nijjaajuq.
I don't like the music.

ᒧᒥᕈᒪᕕᑦ?
mumirumavit?
Do you want to dance?

ᐅᐃᖕᒐᕋᒪ
uirngarama
I'm sleepy.

ᐊᑏ
atii
Let's go.

ᓯᒡᒐᓕᐊᖅᑐᓲᖑᕕᑦ?
siggaliaqtusuunguvit?
Do you smoke?

ᑖᑦᓰᓕᕿᒋᐊᖃᖅᑐᖓ
taatsiiliqigiaqaqtunga
I need to call a taxi.

ᖃᐃᖃᑕᐅᓕᕆᑦ; ᒪᓕᓕᕆᑦ
qaiqataulirit; malilirit
Come along with us.

ᐅᕙᑦᑎᓐᓄᑦ ᒪᓕᒍᒪᕖᑦ?
Uvattinnut maligumaviit?
Do you want to come home with me?

ᐋᒡᒐ, ᖃᖓᑭᐊᖅ ᒪᓕᖔᓛᓕᖅᑯᖓ
Aagga, qangakiaq malingaalaaliqqunga
No, maybe I'll come another time.

ᐋᒡᒐ ᒪᓕᒍᒪᙱᑦᑐᖓ.
Aagga maligumanngittunga.
No, I don't want to go.

ᐊᖏᕐᕋᓕᖅᑐᖓ
angirraliqtunga
I am on my way home.

ᖁᔭᓐᓇᒦᒃ ᐅᓐᓄᖃᑦᑎᐊᕋᒪ.
Qujannamiik unnuqattiarama.
Thanks for the nice evening.

in conversation: **I'm buying**

>> ᑭᓱᒥᒃ ᐱᔪᒪᕕᑦ?
Kisumik pijumavit?
What would you like?

ᐱᐊᒥᒃ <<
piamik
a beer

ᐌᐃᓂᒥᒃ
vainimik
some wine

ᐃᒥᕐᒥᒃ
imirmik
some water

ᑳᐱᒥᒃ
kaapimik
some coffee

>> ᐃᕝᕕᓕᑲᕆᐊᖅ?
ivvillikiaq?
What about you?

ᐊᔾᔨᖓᓂᒃ. <<
ajjinganik.
The same.

>> ᐊᑭᓕᕐᓂᐊᖅᑕᕋ
akilirniaqtara
I'm buying.

ᐋᒡᒐ ᐊᑭᓕᓕᕐᓚᒍ. <<
Aagga akililirlagu.
No, I'll buy.

>> ᒧᒥᕐᓗᒃ
mumirluk
Let's dance.

ᖃᓄᐃᙱᑦᑐᖅ. <<
qanuinngiittuq.
O.K.

ᒧᒥᕈᒪᙱᑦᑐᖓ
mumirumanngittunga
I don't want to dance.

>> ᐃᖏᖓᐊᓕᕐᓗᒃ
ingingaalirluk
Let's sit down.

ᐃᓕᖅᑯᓯᖅ
daily life

an ordinary day
around the house
the office
telephone, computer & e-mail

ᐅᓪᓗᑐᐃᓐᓇᖅ

an ordinary day

IN CONTEXT

For simplicity's sake, the verbs presented below appear in their most basic form. Keep in mind, that in conversation, Inuktitut speakers will use this form of the verb either for an action happening in the present, or one that has happened in the immediate past, depending on the context.

To express the idea of an action that one performs every day, an Inuktitut speaker would normally insert the affix -vat/-pat:

Qautamaat makittapattunga - *I play cards every day.*

ᑐᐸᑦᑐᖓ	tupattunga	*I wake up.*
ᒪᑭᑦᑐᖓ	makittunga	*I get up.*
ᐅᕕᓂᓐᓂᐊᖅᑐᖓ	uvininniaqtunga	*I shower.*
ᐊᓐᓄᕌᖅᑐᖓ	annuraaqtunga	*I get dressed.*
ᑳᐱᓕᐅᖅᑐᖓ	kaapiliuqtunga	*I make coffee.*
ᑳᐱᑐᖅᑐᖓ	kaapituqtunga	*I drink coffee.*
ᓈᓚᐅᑎᑦᑐᖓ	naalautittunga	*I listen to the radio.*
ᓂᕆᔪᖓ	nirijunga	*I eat.*
ᑖᑦᓰᓕᕿᔪᖓ	taatsiiliqijunga	*I call a cab.*
ᐊᓂᔪᖓ	anijunga	*I leave.*
ᐃᖅᑲᓇᐃᔭᕆᐊᖅᑐᖓ	iqqanaijariaqtunga	*I go to work.*
ᐃᖅᑲᓇᐃᔭᖅᑐᖓ	iqqanaijaqtunga	*I work.*
ᑎᑎᖅᑲᓂᐊᕐᕕᒻᒨᖅᑐᖓ	titiqqaniarvimmuuqtunga	*I go to the post office.*
ᓂᕆᔪᖓ ᓂᕆᕕᒻᒥ	nirijunga nirivimmi	*I eat at a restaurant.*
ᐅᑎᖅᑐᖓ ᐊᓪᓚᕝᕕᒻᒧᑦ	utiqtunga allavvimmut	*I return to the office.*
ᐃᖅᑲᓇᐃᔭᒃᑲᓂᖅᑐᖓ	iqqanaijakkaniqtunga	*I work some more.*

ᐱᓕᐅᖅᑐᖓ	tiiliuqtunga	*I make tea.*
ᐱᑐᖅᑐᖓ	tiituqtunga	*I drink tea.*
ᐸᓚᐅᒑᖅᑐᖅᑐᖓ	palaugaaqtuqtunga	*I eat bannock.*
ᐃᖅᑲᓇᐃᔭᕇᖅᑐᖓ	iqqanaijariiqtunga	*I finish working.*
ᓂᐅᕕᕆᐊᖅᑐᖓ	niuviriaqtunga	*I go shopping.*
ᐊᐃᒃᓯᖅᑐᖓ	aiksiqtunga	*I pick something/*
		someone up.
ᐊᖕᒋᕐᕋᐅᔪᖓ	angirraujunga	*I head home.*
ᐃᓯᖅᑐᖓ	isiqtunga	*I go in.*
ᓂᖅᑎᐅᖅᑐᖓ	niqtiuqtunga	*I cook.*
ᐆᔪᖅᑐᖅᑐᖓ	uujuqtuqtunga	*I eat uujuq.*
ᐱᕈᓇᖅᓴᖅᑐᖓ	pirunaqsaqtunga	*I clean up.*
ᐅᖃᓚᔪᖓ	uqaalajunga	*I call someone.*
ᐱᓱᒃᑐᖓ	pisuktunga	*I go for a walk.*
ᐃᖃᓪᓕᐊᖅᑐᖓ	iqalliaqtunga	*I go fishing.*
ᖃᒧᑕᐅᔭᖅᑐᖓ	qamutaujaqtunga	*I go ski-dooing*
ᐅᒥᐊᖅᑐᖅᑐᖓ.	umiaqtuqtunga	*I go boating.*
ᐊᓈᓇᑦᓯᐊᕋ ᐳᓛᖅᑕᕋ	anaanatsiara pulaaqtara	*I visit my grandmother.*
ᕼᐊᑭᖅᑐᖓ	haakiqtunga	*I play hockey.*
ᒧᒥᕆᐊᖅᑐᖓ	mumiriaqtunga	*I go dancing.*
ᒪᑭᑦᑕᖅᑐᖓ	makittaqtunga	*I play cards.*
ᐅᑎᖅᑐᖓ ᐅᕚᑦᑎᓐᓄᑦ	utiqtunga uvattinnut	*I return home.*
ᐅᖃᓕᒫᖅᑐᖓ	uqalimaaqtunga	*I read.*
ᑕᓚᕖᓴᖅᑐᖓ	talaviisaqtunga	*I watch TV.*
ᒥᖅᓱᖅᑐᖓ	miqsuqtunga	*I sew.*
ᐳᓛᖅᑎᖃᖅᑐᖓ	pulaaqtiqaqtunga	*I have a visitor.*
ᐅᐃᕐᖓᖅᑐᖓ	uirngaqtunga	*I am sleepy.*
ᐃᓐᓇᑎᖅᑐᖓ	innatiqtunga	*I go to bed.*
ᓇᓪᓚᖅᑐᖓ	nallaqtunga	*I lie down.*
ᓯᓂᓕᖅᑐᖓ	siniliqtunga	*I fall asleep.*
ᓯᓐᓇᑐᖅᑐᖓ	sinnatuqtunga	*I dream.*

59

ᐃᒡᓗᑉ ᐃᓗᐊᓂᑦᑐᖅ

in the house

ᐃᒡᓗ	illu	*house*
ᐃᒡᓗᕋᕐᓯᖅ	illurusiq	*bedroom*
ᐊᓇᕐᕕᒃ	anarvik	*washroom*
ᑰᖅᑲᕐᕕᒃ	kuuqarvik	*kitchen*
ᐳᓛᕐᕕᒃ	pulaarvik	*living room*
ᓂᕆᕕᒃ	nirivik	*dining room*
ᐊᕙᓗ	avalu	*wall*
ᐃᒐᓛᖅ	igalaaq	*window*
ᒪᔪᕋᐅᑎᑦ	majurautit	*stairs*
ᐹ	paa	*entrance way*
ᒪᑐ / ᐹ	matu / paa	*door*
ᖃᐅᒪᑦ	qaumat	*lights*
ᐃᒐ	iga	*stove*
ᖁᐊᒃᑯᕕᒃ	quakkuvik	*freezer*
ᖁᐊᖃᐅᑦ	quaqaut	*fridge*
ᓵ	saa	*table*
ᖃᐅᒻᒪᖅᑯᑦ	qaummaqqut	*lamp*
ᓯᕐᓗᐊᖅ	sirluaq	*storage shed*

60

ᐃᓪᓘᑉ ᓴᓂᐊᓃᑦᑐᖅ.
Illuup sanianiittuq.
It is beside the house.

ᐃᓪᓗᕈᓯᕐᒦᑦᑐᖓ
illurusirmiittunga
I'm in the bedroom.

ᑰᖃᕐᕕᒦᑦᑐᖓ
kuuqarvimiittunga
I'm in the kitchen.

ᐳᓛᕐᕕᒦᑦᑐᖓ
pulaarvimiittunga
I'm in the living room.

ᐃᑭᒍᒃ
ikiguk
Turn it on.

ᖃᒥᒍᒃ
qamiguk
Turn it off.

ᐃᑯᒪᔪᖅ
ikumajuq
It's turned on.

ᖃᒥᙵᔪᖅ
qaminngajuq
It's turned off.

ᖁᓛᓄᐊᕐᓗᑎᑦ
qulaanuarlutit
Go upstairs.

ᐊᑖᓄᐊᕐᓗᑎᑦ
ataanuarlutit
Go downstairs.

ᖁᓛᓃᑉᐸ?
qulaaniippa?
Is she/he/it upstairs?

ᐃᒐᓛᖅ ᒪᑐᐃᖓᔪᖅ.
Igalaaq matuingajuq.
The window is open.

ᐃᒐᓛᖅ ᒪᑐᐃᑕᖓ.
Igalaaq matuitanga
She / he opens the window.

ᐃᒐᓛᖅ ᒪᑐᐃᕈᒃ.
Igalaaq matuiruk.
Open the window.

ᐃᒐᓛᖅ ᒪᑐᓯᒪᔪᖅ.
Igalaaq matusimajuq.
The window is closed.

ᐃᒐᓛᖅ ᒪᑐᒍᒃ.
Igalaaq matuguk.
Close the window.

ᓈᓚᐅᑦ ᓂᐱᖅᑯᑐᓯᒋᐊᕈᒃ
ᑐᓵᙱᓇᒃᑯ!
Naalaut nipiqqutusigiaruk
tusaannginakku!
Turn up the radio, I can't hear!

ᓈᓚᐅᑦ ᓂᐱᑭᓪᓕᒋᐊᕈᒃ,
ᓂᐱᖅᑯᖅᑐᓗᐊᕐᒪᑦ!
Naalaut nipikilligiaruk,
nipiqquqtuluarmat !
Turn down the radio, it's too loud!

ᐅᖅᑰᓴᐅᑦ ᐃᑭᒋᐊᕈᒃ.
Uqquusaut ikigiaruk.
Turn the heat up.

ᐅᖅᑰᓴᐅᑦ ᖃᒥᒋᐊᕈᒃ.
Uqquusaut qamigiaruk.
Turn the heat down.

ᓴᓗᒻᒪᖅᓴᐃᒋᑦ
salummaqsaigit
Please clean up.

>> ᓇᒦᑉᐹ ᓇᒻᒪᒑᕋ?
Namiippa nammagaara?
Where is my knapsack?

ᐊᑦᓲ.
Aatsuu. <<
I don't know.

ᐃᓪᓗᕉᓯᓐᓃᑦᑐᖅ.
illurusinniittuq.
It's in my bedroom.

ᑰᖅᑲᕐᕕᒦᑦᑐᖅ.
Kuuqarvimiittuq.
It's in the kitchen.

ᓯᓚᒦᑦᑐᖅ.
Silamiittuq.
It's outside.

>> ᓱᑯᑦᑎᐊᓃᑉᐹ?
Sukuttianiippa?
Where exactly is it?

ᐃᓪᓕᑉᐵ ᐊᑖᓂ.
illiqpit ataani. <<
Under your bed.

ᐃᑦᓯᕚᐅᑕᐅᑉ ᖃᖔᓃᑦᑐᖅ.
Itsivautaup qaanganiittuq.
It's on the chair.

>> ᐃᓪᓗᕉᓰᑦ ᓴᓗᒻᒪᖅᓴᕈᒃ.
illurusiit salummaqsaruk.
Please clean up your room.

ᓇᒦᒻᒪᑕ ᓴᓂᐅᑏᑦ?
Namiimmata saniutiit? <<
Where's the broom?

>> ᓴᓂᒃᑯᕕᒃ ᑕᑕᑦᑐᖅ.
Sanikkuvik tatattuq.
The garbage is full.

ᓴᓂᒃᑯᕕᒃ ᐊᓂᒍᒃ.
Sanikkuvik aniguk. <<
Go throw out the garbage.

ᐊᑦᑕᕐᕕᒃ

the office

INUKTITUT AS A LANGUAGE OF WORK

Since the creation of Nunavut, Inuktitut has made important advances as a language of the workplace. It is the main language of work among Nunavut's politicians in the Legislative Assembly and is regularly used throughout the government. A new law, meanwhile, the Inuit Language Protection Act, enshrines the right of public servants to perform their duties in Inuktitut.

Some of the barriers to using Inuktitut effectively in an office environment have also been overcome. Inuktitut continues to adopt new terminology to match new terms that appear in English. Computer technology has also evolved new ways of incorporating syllabics. And, Microsoft's most popular software and operating systems can now be used in Inuktitut.

ᐊᑦᑕᕐᕕᒃ	allavvik	*office*
ᑎᑎᖅᑲᑦ	titiqqat	*letters; documents*
ᑎᑎᕋᐅᑦ	titiraut	*pen; pencil*
ᐸᐃᑉᐹᖅ	paippaaq	*paper*
ᐊᑦᑕᕈᔮᒃ	allirujaak	*scissors*
ᑭᑭᐊᑦᓯᔾᔪᑦ	kikiatsijjut	*stapler*
ᐅᖃᓕᒫᒐᒃᑯᕕᒃ	uqalimaagakkuvik	*book shelf*
ᓱᒃᑲᔪᒃᑰᕈᑦ	sukkajukkuurut	*fax machine*
ᐊᒥᓱᓕᐅᕈᑦ	amisuliurut	*photo copier*
ᐸᐃᑉᐹᒨᕆᔾᔪᑦ	paippaamuurijjut	*printer*
ᖃᕋᓴᐅᔭᖅ	qarasaujaq	*computer*
ᖃᕋᓴᐅᔭᕋᓛᖅ	qarasaujaralaaq	*laptop*
ᑲᑎᒪᕕᒃ	katimavik	*boardroom*
ᐃᓂᓴᖅ	inissaq	*appointment*

ᐱᔭᔅᓴᖃᓗᐊᖅᐱᑦ?
pijassaqaluaqpit?
Are you too busy?

ᐃᖅᑲᓇᐃᔭᕆᓯᒪ
iqqanaijariiruma
when I am done work

ᐱᔭᔅᓴᖃᓗᐊᖅᑐᖓ
pijassaqaluaqtunga
I am very busy.

ᖃᐅᑉᐸᑦ ᑭᖑᕙᓛᖅᑐᖓ.
Qauppat kinguvalaaqtunga.
I'll be late tomorrow

ᓱᓕ ᐱᓕᕆᔪᖓ.
Suli pilirijunga.
I'm still busy.

ᑲᑎᒪᔪᑦ
katimajut
They are meeting.

ᐱᓕᕆᔭᕋ
pilirijara
I am working on it.

ᐅᓪᓗᒥ ᑲᑎᒪᖃᑎᒋᔪᓐᓇᖅᐱᒋᑦ?
Ullumi katimaqatigijunnaqpigit?
Can you meet with me today?

ᐱᔭᕇᓪᓚᕆᓕᕋᓗᐊᖅᑐᖓ
pijariillariliraluaqtunga
I am almost done.

ᑲᑎᒪᔪᓐᓇᕐᓂᐊᖅᑐᒍᒃ
katimajunnarniaqtuguk.
We two can meet later today.

ᖃᐅᑉᐸᖅᑲᐃ ᐱᔭᕇᓛᓕᖅᑕᒃᑲ.
Qauppaqqai pijariilaaliqtakka.
I might be done by tomorrow.

ᑲᑎᒪᔭᖅᑐᕆᐊᖃᕋᒪ
katimajaqturiaqarama
I have to go to a meeting.

ᐱᔭᕇᖅᓯᒪᔪᖅ
pijariiqsimajuq
It is ready; it is finished.

ᑭᖑᕙᖅᑲᐅᔪᖓ
kinguvaqqaujunga
I've arrived late (for a meeting).

ᑎᑎᕋᐅᑎᖃᖅᐱᑦ?
titirautiqaqpit?
Do you have a pen?

ᑲᑎᒪᔭᖅᑐᖅᓵᓕᔪᖓ
katimajaqtuqsaalijunga
I'm early (for a meeting).

ᐊᑎᓕᐅᖅᑕᕋ
atiliuqtara
I signed it.

ᐃᖏᑦᑎᐊᕆᑦ
ingittiarit
Please sit down.

ᐃᓂᔅᓴᓕᐅᖅᑐᖅ
inissaliuqtuq
She/he makes an appointment.

ᑳᐱᑕᖃᖅᐹ?
kaapitaqaqpa?
Is there any coffee?

ᐃᖅᑲᓇᐃᔭᖅᑐᖅ
iqqanaijaqtuq
She / he is working.

ᑳᐱᑕᓕᒃ.
kaapitalik.
There's coffee made.

in conversation: **where do you work?**

» ᓇᒥ ᐃᖅᑲᓇᐃᔭᖅᐱᑦ?
Nami iqqanaijaqpit?
Where do you work?

ᒪᓕᒐᓕᕆᔨᒃᑯᓐᓂ ᐃᖅᑲᓇᐃᔭᖅᑐᖓ.
Maligalirijikkunni iqqanaijaqtunga.
I work at the Dept. of Justice. «

ᐃᓕᓐᓂᐊᖅᑐᓕᕆᔨᒃᑯᓐᓂ
ᐃᖅᑲᓇᐃᔭᖅᑐᖓ.
Ilinniaqtulirijikkunni iqqanaijaqtunga.
I work at the Dept. of Education.

ᓰᐲᓰᒃᑯᓐᓂ ᐃᖅᑲᓇᐃᔭᖅᑐᖓ.
CBC-kkunni iqqanaijaqtunga.
I work at CBC.

Hᐋᒪᓚᒃᑯᓐᓂ ᐃᖅᑲᓇᐃᔭᖅᑐᖓ.
Haamalakkunni iqqanaijaqtunga.
I work at the Hamlet (municipal) office.

» ᑭᓱᓕᕆᔨᐅᒐᕕᓪᓕ?
Kisulirijiugavilli?
And what do you do?

ᑐᑭᒧᐊᑎᑦᓯᔨᐅᔪᖓ.
Tukimuatitsijiujunga.
I am a director. «

ᐃᓕᓴᐃᔨᐅᔪᖓ.
ilisaijiujunga.
I am a teacher.

ᓄᑭᓪᓚᐅᓯᕆᔨᐅᔪᖓ.
Nukillausirijiujunga.
I am an electrician.

ᖃᑦᑎᕆᔨᐅᔪᖓ.
Qattirijiujunga.
I am a firefighter.

» ᐃᖅᑲᓇᐃᔮᑦ ᖁᕕᐊᒋᕕᐅᒃ?
Iqqanaijaat quviagiviuk?
Do you like your job?

ᖁᕕᐊᒋᔭᕋ ᐃᖅᑲᓇᐃᔮᕋ.
Quviagijara iqqanaijaara.
I like what I do at work. «

ᐅᖄᓚᐅᑦ, ᖃᕐᓴᐅᔮᖅ
ᐃᕐᖁᒥᖁᖅᑕᐅᒡᓗ

phone, computer & e-mail

ELECTRONIC INUKTITUT

Office communications in Inuktitut took a big leap forward in the 1970s with the development of the first electric typewriter accessories for syllabics. With the advent of e-mail, many Inuktitut speakers used roman orthography, a situation that is changing as computer software becomes more syllabic-friendly.

Since 2004 a major effort has been underway to develop Inuktitut versions of popular software including Microsoft Windows XP & Vista as well as Microsoft Office 2003 and 2007.

A sample of the vocabulary adapted for these software appears in the pages that follow. Inuktitut software is available for free via Microsoft's website.

As with English computer vocabulary, many terms are commonly used words, while others have been created for a very specific computer context.

And then, there's always the old-fashioned telephone. As with daily conversation, discussions on the telephone in Inuktitut take place without a lot of the polite language and niceties used in English and French.

ᐅᖄᓚᐅᑦ	uqaalaut	*telephone*
ᐅᖄᓚᐅᑎᕋᓛᖅ	uqaalautiralaaq	*cell phone*
ᐅᖄᓚᐅᑎᓯᐅᑏᑦ	uqaalautisiutiit	*phone book*
ᐅᖄᓚᔪᖅ	uqaalajuq	*He/she is phoning.*
ᐅᖄᓚᕕᒋᓂᐊᖅᑕᕋ	uqaalaviginiaqtara	*I will call him.*
ᐅᖄᓚᕕᒋᔭᕇᖅᑕᕋ	uqaalavigijariiqtara	*I already called him.* *(immediate past)*
ᐅᖄᓚᕕᒋᖅᑲᐅᔭᕋ	uqaalavigiqqaujara	*I already called him.* *(earlier today)*

computer terms

ᖃᕋᓴᐅᔭᖅ	qarasaujaq	*computer*
ᖃᕋᓴᐅᔭᕋᓛᖅ	qarasaujaralaaq	*laptop*
ᐃᒐᓛᖑᔭᖅ	igalaangujaq	*screen; monitor*
ᓇᕿᑦᑕᐅᑦ	naqittaut	*keyboard*
ᐊᕕᙵᙳᐊᖅ	avinngannguaq	*mouse*
ᓯᐅᒻᒥᒑᒃ	siummigaak	*headphones*
ᑐᖅᑰᒪᕕᒃ	tuqquumavik	*hard drive; drive; disk*
ᕿᓪᓕᖅᑐᖅ	qilliqtuq	*CD (compact disk)*
ᐃᑭᐊᖅᑭᔾᔪᑦ	ikiaqqijjut	*internet*
ᐃᑭᐊᖅᑭᕕᒃ	ikiaqqivik	*World Wide Web*
ᐃᑭᐊᖅᑭᕕᒃᑯᑦ ᑐᑭᓯᒋᐊᕐᕕᒃ	ikiaqqivikkut tukisigiarvik	*website*
ᐃᓂ	ini	*file*
ᐴᕐᕕᒃ	puurvik	*folder*
ᐃᒐᓚᐅᔭᖅ	igalaujaq	*desktop*
ᑎᑎᖅᑲᖅ	titiqqaq	*document*
ᒪᑐᐃᕐᓕ	matuirli	*open*
ᒪᑐᓕ	matuli	*close*
ᔭᒐᔾᔭᐃᕐᓕ	jagajjairli	*save*
ᐊᑦᑎᕐᓕ ᐃᒫᒃ	attirli imaak	*save as*
ᐲᕐᓕ	piirli	*delete*
ᐸᐃᑉᐹᒨᕐᓕ	paippaamuurli	*print*
ᓇᑲᓪᓕ	nakalli	*cut*
ᐃᔾᔪᐊᕐᓕ	ijjuarli	*copy*
ᓂᐱᑎᓪᓕ	nipitilli	*paste*
ᑎᑎᕋᐅᓯᖅ	titirausiq	*font*
ᐊᑐᖅᑐᖅ	atuqtuq	*user*
ᐃᓯᕈᑦ	isirut	*password*
ᓄᖅᑲᖓᓕ	nuqqangali	*logoff*
ᐃᓯᕆᑦ	isirit	*logon*
ᖃᒥᓪᓕ	qamilli	*shutdown*

e-mail

ᐃᕐᖏᓈᖅᑕᐅᑦ	irngiinaaqtaut	*email*
ᓇᔅᓯᐅᑎᓕ	nassiutili	*send*
ᓇᔅᓯᐅᔾᔪᓯᐊᖅ	nassiujjusiaq	*receive*
ᑭᐅᓕ	kiuli	*reply*
ᓯᕗᒧᑦ	sivumut	*forward*
ᑎᑎᖅᑲᐅᓯᐊᕐᕕᒃ	titiqqausiarvik	*inbox*
ᓇᔅᓯᐅᑎᓯᒪᔪᑦ	nassiutisimajut	*sent items*
ᒥᑦᓵᓄᑦ	mitsaanut	*RE:*
ᖃᐅᔨᒪᖁᓪᓗᑏᑦ	qaujimaqullutit	*FYI (I want you to let know)*

e-mail auto-reply

ᐅᓪᓗᒥ ᐊᓪᓚᕕᒻᒦᒃᑲᓗᐊᖅᑐᖓ.
Ullumi allavimmiikkaluaqtunga.
I am in the office today.

ᒪᐃ 14-ᙳᕋᓱᐊᕐᓂᖓᓂ ᐊᓪᓚᕕᒻᒦᔾᔮᖏᓐᓇᒪ.
Mai 14-nngurasuarningani allavimmiijjaanginnama.
I will be away from the office until May 14.

ᐃᕐᖏᓈᖅᑕᐅᑏᑦ ᖃᐅᔨᒋᐊᖅᑕᕐᓂᐊᖅᑕᒃᑲ.
Irngiinaaqtautit qaujigiaqattarniaqtakka.
I will be checking e-mails.

ᐃᕐᖏᓈᖅᑕᐅᑏᑦ ᖃᐅᔨᒋᐊᖅᑕᴊᔮᖏᑕᒃᑲ.
Irngiinaaqtautit qaujigiaqattajjaangitakka.
I will not be checking e-mails.

ᐃᑲᔪᖅᑕᐅᔪᒪᒍᕕᑦ, ᐅᕗᖓ ᖃᐅᔨᒋᐊᕈᓐᓇᖅᑐᑎᑦ....
Ikajuqtaujumaguvit, uvunga qaujigiarunnaqtutit...
For assistance, please contact...

telephone: voicemail phrases

Peter Smith-ᒧᑦ ᐅᖄᓚᔪᑎᑦ.
Peter Smith-mut uqaalajutit.
You have reached Peter Smith.

ᒫᓐᓇ ᐅᖄᓚᐅᑦ ᑭᐅᔪᓐᓇᖏᓐᓇᒃᑯ.
Maanna uqaalaut kiujunnanginnakku.
I can't answer the phone right now.

ᓂᐱᓕᐅᕈᓐᓇᖅᑐᑎᑦ
Nipiliurunnaqtutit.
Please leave me a message.

ᐅᓪᓗᒥ ᐊᓪᓚᕕᒻᒦᒃᑲᓗᐊᖅᑐᖓ.
Ullumi allavimmiikkaluaqtunga.
I am in the office today.

ᒫᓐᓇ ᐊᓪᓚᕕᒻᒦᖏᓐᓇᒪ.
Maanna allavimmiinginnama.
I am not in the office.

ᒪᐃ 14-ᙵᖃᓯᐊᖅᓂᖓᓂ ᐊᓪᓚᕕᒻᒦᔾᔮᖏᓐᓇᒪ.
Mai 14-nngurasuarningani allavimmiijjaanginnama.
I will be away from the office until May 14.

ᐅᖅᑲᖅᕕᖅᑲᑦᑕᐅᑎᒋᔪᒪᒍᕕᑦ ᐅᖄᓚᕕᒋᔪᓐᓇᖅᑕᐃᑦ ᒥᐊᓕ ᔫᓇᓯᒧᑦ.
Uqarviqattautigijumaguvit uqaalavigijunnaqtait Miali Juunasi-mut.
To speak to someone right away please call Miali Juunasi.

ᐊᓪᓚᑦᑎᒥᒃ ᐅᖅᑲᖅᕕᖅᑲᑦᑕᐅᑎᒋᔪᒪᒍᕕᑦ ᔩᐅᓗ ᓇᖅᑭᓪᓗᒍ.
Allattimik uqarviqattautigijumaguvit jiulu naqillugu.
To speak to the receptionist, please press zero.

ᐱᔪᓐᓇᖅᓯᑐᐊᕈᒪ ᐅᖄᓚᕕᒋᓂᐊᖃᒃᑭᑦ
Pijunnaqsituaruma uqaalaviginiarakkit.
I'll call you when I can.

ᖁᔭᓐᓇᒦᒃ, ᐅᓪᓗᖅᑲᑦᑎᐊᕆᑦ.
Qujannamiik, ulluqattiarit.
Thank you and have a good day.

in conversation: **on the phone**

>> ᐱᑕ ᑕᕝᕙᓃᑉᐸ?
Piita tavvaniippa?
Is Peter there?

ᐃ, ᐅᕙᓃᑦᑐᖅ. <<
ii, uvaniittuq.
Yes, he's here.

>> ᐅᖃᐊᓚᕕᒋᓚᒍ
Uqaalavigilagu
Let me speak to him.

ᐅᖃᐊᓚᕕᒋᒍᒃ? <<
Uqaalavigiguk?
Do you want to speak with him?

ᐅᐊᑦᓯᐊᕈᐊᐃ / ᓯᐊᕈᐊᐃ <<
uatsiaruai / siaruai
Just a moment.

ᐋᒡᒐ, ᐅᕙᓃᖕᖏᑦᑐᖅ. <<
Aagga, uvaniinngittuq.
No, he's not here.

ᐊᓂᑲᐃᓐᓇᖅᓯᒪᔪᖅ. <<
Anikainnaqsimajuq.
He has stepped out.

>> ᐊᐅᓪᓚᖅᓯᒪᕚ?
Aullaqsimavaa?
Is she out of town?

ᐊᐅᓪᓚᖅᓯᒪᔪᖅ. <<
Aullaqsimajuq.
She's out of town.

>> ᐅᖃᐊᓚᖁᕕᐅᒃ?
Uqaalaquviuk?
Do you want him to call you?

ᐅᕓᓄᑦ
ᐅᖃᐊᓚᖁᔪᓐᓇᖅᐱᐅᒃ? <<
Uvannut
uqaalaqujunnaqpiuk?
Can you have him call me?

>> ᑭᓇᐅᕚᑦ?
Kinaugavit?
What's your name?

ᐃᓕᓴᐱᐅᔪᖓ. <<
Ilisapiujunga.
This is Ilisapi.

>> ᐅᖃᐊᓚᐅᑏᑦ ᖃᑦᑎᐅᒻᒪᑦ?
Uqaalautit qattiummat?
What's your phone number?

ᐅᖃᐊᓚᐅᑎᒐ 979-0000 <<
Uqaalautiga 979-0000.
My number is 979-0000.

70

ᓄᓇᓕᑦᑎᓂ

in town

inuit communities
where are you off to?
shopping

photo: Nunavut Tourism

ᐃᓄᐃᑦ ᓄᓇᓕᖏᑦ

inuit communities

IS IT IGLOOLIK OR IGLULIK?

Unlike their counterparts in Nunavik and Greenland, communities in Nunavut are not required by law to use their Inuktitut names. The decision of whether to use Inuktitut or English for the official name rests with municipal government.

Since 1984, seven communities (Iqaluit, Qikiqtarjuaq, Arviat, Kugluktuk, Kimmirut, Taloyoak and Kugaaruk) have changed their official names from English to Inuktitut. Others, like Igloolik and Pangnirtung, have always been known by their Inuktitut name.

Note that in English, a number of communities (Kugluktuk, Taloyoak, Igloolik, Pangnirtung) use older spellings of their Inuit names. Hence the spellings do not match those that are used in modern standardized Inuktitut.

qikiqtaaluk

ᕿᑭᖅᑖᓗᒃ	Qikiqtaaluk	*Baffin Island*
ᐊᐅᓱᐃᑦᑐᖅ	Ausuittuq	*Grise Fiord*
ᐃᒡᓗᓕᒃ	Iglulik	*Igloolik*
ᐃᒃᐱᐊᕐᔪᒃ	Ikpiarjuk	*Arctic Bay*
ᐃᖃᓗᐃᑦ	Iqaluit	*Iqaluit*
ᑲᖏᖅᑐᒑᐱᒃ	Kangiqtugaapik	*Clyde River*
ᑭᒻᒥᕈᑦ	Kimmirut	*Kimmirut*
ᑭᙵᐃᑦ	Kinngait	*Cape Dorset*
ᒥᑦᑎᒪᑕᓕᒃ	Mittimatalik	*Pond Inlet*
ᓂᐊᖁᙳᑦ	Niaqunnguut	*Apex*
ᐸᓐᓂᖅᑑᖅ	Panniqtuuq	*Pangnirtung*
ᖃᐅᓱᐃᑦᑐᖅ	Qausuittuq	*Resolute Bay*
ᕿᑭᖅᑕᕐᔪᐊᖅ	Qikiqtarjuaq	*Qikiqtarjuaq*
ᓴᓂᑭᓗᐊᖅ	Sanikiluaq	*Sanikiluaq*
ᓴᓂᕋᔭᒃ	Sanirajak	*Hall Beach*

kivalliq

ᐊᕐᕕᐊᑦ	Arviat	*Arviat*
ᐃᒡᓗᓕᒑᕐᔪᒃ	Igluligaarjuk	*Chesterfield Inlet*
ᑲᖏᕐᖠᓂᕐᖅ	Kangiqtiniq	*Rankin Inlet*
ᖃᒪᓂᑦᑐᐊᕐᖅ	Qamani'tuaq	*Baker Lake*
ᓇᐅᔮᑦ	Naujaat	*Repulse Bay*
ᓴᓪᓖᑦ	Salliit	*Coral Harbour*
ᑎᑭᕋᕐᔪᐊᕐᖅ	Tikirarjuaq	*Whale Cove*
ᐊᐃᕕᓕᒃ	Aivilik	*coast from Chesterfield Inlet to Repulse Bay*

qitirmiut

ᕐᑭᑎᕐᒥᐅᑦ	Qitirmiut	*Kitikmeot Region*
ᐃᕐᖃᓗᒃᑑᑦᑎᐊᕐᖅ	Iqaluktuuttiaq	*Cambridge Bay*
ᑰᒑᕐᔪᒃ	Kuugaarjuk	*Kugaaruk*
ᕐᑭᖕᐅᑦ	Qingaut	*Bathurst Inlet*
ᕐᑯᕐᓗᕐᖅᑐᕐᖅ	Qurluqtuq	*Kugluktuk*
ᑕᓗᕐᔪᐊᕐᖅ	Talurjuaq	*Taloyoak*
ᐅᒥᖕᒪᒃᑑᕐᖅ	Umingmaktuuq	*Umingmaktok*
ᐅᕐᖅᓱᕐᖁᕐᖅ	Uqhuqtuuq	*Gjoa Haven*
ᓇᑦᓯᓕᒃ	Natsilik	*coast from Kugaaruk to Gjoa Haven*

ukiuqtaqtuq

ᐅᑭᐅᕐᖅᑕᕐᖅᑐᕐᖅ	Ukiuqtaqtuq	*The Arctic*
ᐊᑯᐱᑦᑐᕐᖅ	Akukittuq	*Greenland*
ᓄᓇᑦᓯᐊᕗᑦ	Nunatsiavut	*Labrador*
ᓄᓇᕕᒃ	Nunavik	*Nunavik*
ᓄᓇᑦᓯᐊᕐᖅ	Nunatsiaq	*Northwest Territories*

ᓇᒍᖕᒪᓕᑦᖃᐱᑦ?

where are you off to?

ᓄᓇᓕᒃ	nunalik	*community*
ᐃᓕᓐᓂᐊᕐᕕᒃ	ilinniarvik	*school*
ᐸᐃᕆᕕᒃ	pairivik	*daycare*
ᐋᓐᓂᐊᕕᒃ	aanniavik	*hospital; nursing station*
ᐃᖅᑲᖅᑐᐃᕕᒃ	iqqaqtuivik	*courthouse*
ᑎᑎᖅᑲᓂᐊᕐᕕᒃ	titiqqaniarvik	*post office*
ᐱᙳᐊᖅ	pinnguaq	*game*
ᐱᙳᐊᕐᕕᒃ	pinnguarvik	*recreational centre*
ᓴᐊᑭᕐᕕᒃ	haakirvik	*hockey arena*
ᑐᑦᓯᐊᖅᑐᖅ	tutsiaqtuq	*he / she prays*
ᑐᑦᓯᐊᕐᕕᒃ	tutsiarvik	*church*
ᑕᑯᔭᒐᖃᕐᕕᒃ	takujagaqarvik	*museum*
ᓈᓚᐅᑎᖃᕐᕕᒃ	naalautiqarvik	*radio station*
ᓯᐱᐃᓰᒃᑯᑦ	siipiisiikkut	*CBC station*
ᖃᑦᑎᕆᔨ	qattiriji	*firefighter*
ᖃᑦᑎᕆᔨᒃᑯᑦ	qattirijikkut	*fire hall*
ᐸᓖᓯ	paliisi	*police*
ᐸᓖᓯᒃᑯᑦ	paliisikkut	*police department*
ᒥᕐᖑᐃᖅᓯᕐᕕᒃ	mirnguiqsirvik	*park*
ᓂᐅᕕᖅᑐᖅ	niuviqtuq	*she / he buys*
ᓂᐅᕕᕐᕕᒃ	niuvirvik	*store*

ᓂᐅᕕᕐᕕᕋᓛᖅ	niuvirviralaaq	*corner store*
ᐃᖃᓗᒃᑖᕐᕕᒃ	iqaluktaarvik	*fish store*
ᐅᖅᓱᐊᓗᒃ	uqsualuk	*gasoline*
ᐅᖅᓱᐊᓗᒃᑖᕐᕕᒃ	uqsualuktaarvik	*gas station*
ᐄᔭᒐᖅ	iijagaq	*pill*
ᐄᔭᒐᖅᑖᕐᕕᒃ	iijagaqtaarvik	*pharmacy*
ᑭᒍᓐᓂᐊᕐᕕᒃ	kigunniarvik	*dentist's office*
ᑮᓇᐅᔭᖅ	kiinaujaq	*money*
ᑮᓇᐅᔭᒃᑯᕕᒃ	kiinaujakkuvik	*bank*
ᒪᑐᐃᖓᔪᖅ	matuingajuq	*It is open.*
ᒪᑐᓯᒪᔪᖅ	matusimajuq	*It is closed.*
ᑳᐱᑐᕐᕕᒃ	kaapiturvik	*coffee shop*
ᓂᕆᕕᒃ	nirivik	*restaurant*
ᑐᔪᕐᒥᕕᒃ	tujurmivik	*hotel*
ᐃᒥᕋᓚᕝᕕᒃ	imiralavvik	*bar*
ᑕᕐᕆᔭᕐᕕᒃ	tarrijarvik	*movie theatre*
ᐃᓪᓗᐃᑦ ᐊᓪᓚᕝᕖᑦ	illuit allavviit	*office building*
ᐃᓪᓗᐃᑦ ᐊᑕᔪᑦ	illuit atajut	*apartment building*
ᐃᓪᓗᐊᓗᒃ	illualuk	*High Rise (Iqaluit)*
ᖁᓛ ᓯᕗᓪᓕᖅ	qulaa sivulliq	*first floor*
ᖁᓛ ᑭᖑᓪᓕᖅ	qulaa kingulliq	*second floor*
ᐃᓪᓗᑯᑖᑦ	illukutaat	*row house*
ᐊᖅᑯᑦ	aqqut	*street*
ᓄᖅᑲᕐᕕᒃ	nuqqarvik	*stop sign*
ᓄᖅᑲᕆᑦ!	nuqqarit!	*stop!*
ᖃᖓᑕᓲᖅ	qangatasuuq	*airplane*
ᖃᖓᑕᓲᒃᑯᕕᒃ	qangatasuukkuvik	*airport*
ᓱᑯᑦᑎᐊᓃᒻᒪᑦ ᑎᑎᖅᑲᓂᐊᕐᕕᒃ?	sukuttianiimmat titiqqaniarvik?	*Where exactly is the post office?*
ᓇᒧᙵᓕᖅᐱᑦ	namunngaliqpit?	*Where are you off to?*
ᒫᓐᓇ ᓇᒦᑉᐱᑦ?	Maanna namiippit?	*Where are you right now?*

in conversation: **where are you?**

>> ᓇᒦᑉᐱᑦ?
Namiippit?
Where are you?

ᐅᕙᑦᑎᓐᓂ. <<
Uvattinni.
At home.

ᐊᓪᓚᕝᕕᒻᒥ.
Allavvimmi.
At the office.

ᐃᓚᑦᑎᓐᓂ.
ilattinni.
At my relatives' place.

>> ᓇᒧᙵᖅᐱᑦ?
Namunngaqpit?
Where are you going?

ᐅᕙᑦᑎᓐᓄᑦ. <<
Uvattinnut.
(to) Home.

ᐊᓪᓚᕝᕕᒻᒧᑦ.
Allavvimmut
To the office.

ᑎᑎᖅᑲᓂᐊᕐᕕᒻᒨᖅᑐᖓ.
Titiqqaniarvimmuuqtunga.
I'm going to the post office.

ᓂᐅᕕᕆᐊᖅᑐᖓ.
Niuviriaqtunga.
I am going shopping.

>> ᓇᑭᙵᐊᖅᐱᑦ?
Nakinngaaqpit?
Where are you coming (back) from?

ᐅᕙᑦᑎᓐᓂᑦ. <<
Uvattinnit.
From home.

ᐱᙳᐊᕕᒻᒥᙵᐊᖅᑐᒍᑦ.
Pinnguavimminngaaqtugut.
We are coming from the rec centre.

ᓂᐅᕕᕐᓂᖅ

shopping

IN CONTEXT

The style and skill of Inuit artists and sewers are recognized around the world. Residents and visitors to Nunavut have the opportunity to see and often buy an incredible variety of hand made goods. Many communities have local specialties (woven baskets from Sanikiluaq) or unique styles (the surreal figures in Natsilingmiut carvings). Sewing continues to be an important occupation throughout Nunavut.

In the larger communities, there are specialty stores carrying hand made goods from all over the territory. In some communities artists are organized and sell their work through their print shop. Elsewhere, locally produced goods are usually available through the Co-op or Northern store.

Another option throughout Nunavut is to buy goods directly from sewers and artists, often at their home.

ᓂᐅᕕᕐᕕᒃ	niuvirvik	*store*
ᐄᔭᒐᖅᑖᕐᕕᒃ	iijagaqtaarvik	*pharmacy*
ᐃᖃᓗᒃᑖᕐᕕᒃ	iqaluktaarvik	*fish store*
ᑕᑯᔭᒐᖃᕐᕕᒃ	takujagaqarvik	*museum*
ᒪᑐᓯᒪᔪᖅ	matusimajuq	*It's closed.*
ᒪᑐᐃᖓᔪᖅ	matuingajuq	*It's open.*
ᐊᑭᖓ	akinga	*price*
ᐊᑭᑭᑦᑐᖅ	akikittuq	*cheap*
ᐊᑭᑐᔪᖅ	akitujuq	*expensive*
ᑮᓇᐅᔭᖅ	kiinaujaq	*money*
ᖁᕕᐊᓲᓯᐊᖅ	quviasuusiaq	*Christmas present*
ᓄᓇᕋᐃᑦ	nunarait	*flowers*
ᐅᖃᓕᒫᒐᖅ	uqalimaagaq	*book*
ᕿᓪᓕᖅᑐᖅ	qilliqtuq	*CD (compact disk)*

77

carvings

ᓴᓇᙱᐅᐊᒐᖅ	sanannguagaq	*carving*
ᓇᔾᔪᒃ	najjuk	*antler*
ᑑᒑᖅ	tuugaaq	*ivory*
ᑯᔭᐱᒐᖅ	kujapigaq	*whale vertebrae*
ᑎᑎᖅᑐᒐᖅ	titiqtugaq	*print*
ᐊᕙᓗᒥᐅᑕᖅ	avalumiutaq	*wall hanging*

jewelry

ᑕᑯᒥᓇᖅᓴᐅᑎᑦ	takuminaqsautit	*jewelry*
ᒎᓗ	guulu	*gold*
ᓯᐅᒻᒥᐅᑖᒃ	siummiutaak	*earrings*
ᐅᔭᒥᒃ	ujamik	*necklace*
ᑕᓕᐊᙱᐊᖅ	taliannguaq	*bracelet*
ᓇᒡᒍᐊᕐᒥᒃ	nagguarmik	*ring*

clothing

ᐊᓐᓄᕌᑦ	annuraat	*clothing*
ᐊᑯᖅ	akuq	*amauti (long tailed style)*
ᐊᖏᔪᖅᑕᐅᔭᖅ	angijuqtaujaq	*amauti (skirted style)*
ᖃᒃᓱᖕᒑᐅᑦ	qaksungaut	*tie for the amauti*
ᑲᒦᒃ	kamiik	*skin boots*
ᓇᓴᖅ	nasaq	*hat*
ᐳᐊᓘᒃ	pualuuk	*mitts*
ᖃᕐᓕᑲᓪᓛᒃ	qarlikallaak	*skin pants*
ᖁᓕᑦᑕᐅᔭᖅ	qulittaujaq	*parka (contemporary)*
ᐅᐊᓯᑯᐊᖅ	uasikuaq	*vest*

dealing with artists and sewers

ᑭᓱᕋᔭᒃ ᐅᓇ?
Kisurajak una?
What is this made of?

ᐅᓇ ᓇᔾᔪᒃ?
Una najjuk?
Is this antler?

ᐅᓇ ᑑᒑᖅ?
Una tuugaaq?
Is this ivory?

ᐅᓇ ᑭᓱᕋᔭᒃ?
Una kisurajak?
What kind of skin/fur is it?

ᕿᓯᒃ
qisik
seal skin

ᐊᒥᖅ
amiq
caribou skin

ᑎᕆᒑᓂᐊᕋᔭᒃ
tiriganiarajak
fox fur

ᓇᓄᕋᖅ
nanuraq
polar bear fur

ᖃᕝᕕᕋᔭᒃ
qavvirajak
wolverine fur

ᐅᒥᒻᒪᕋᔭᒃ
umimmarajak
muskox wool

ᐅᓇ ᓴᓇᔭᒥᓃᑦ?
Una sanajaminiit?
Did you make this?

ᑭᐊᑉ ᓴᓇᔭᖓ?
Kiap sanajanga?
Who made this?

ᓇᒥ ᓴᓇᔭᒥᓂᖅ?
Nami sanajaminiq?
Where was it made?

ᖃᑦᓯᕌᕐᒪᑦ?
qatsiraarmat?
How much?

ᓈᒻᒪᑦᑐᖅ
naammattuq
O.K., that's good.

ᖁᓕᑦᑕᐅᔭᓕᐅᕈᑎᙵ?
qulittaujaliurutinnga?
Could you make me a parka?

ᑲᒻᒥᐅᕈᓐᓇᖅᐱᖓ?
kammiurunnaqpinga?
Could you make me some kamiik?

ᖃᓄᖅ ᐊᑯᓂᐅᑎᒋᓂᐊᖅᐸ?
Qanuq akuniutiginiaqpa?
How long will it take?

ᖃᑦᓯᕌᕐᓂᐊᖅᐸ?
qatsiraarniaqpa?
How much will it cost?

ᐱᔭᕇᖅᓯᒪᔪᖅ
pijariiqsimajuq
It's finished.

in town : shopping

environment

weather
land & water
animals
hunting
food
camping

photo: Leena Evic

ᓯᓚ

weather

SILA & QILAK

*The term **sila** is used to describe a number of concepts in English, including weather and the environment. This word has its roots in traditional Inuit perceptions of the universe that saw weather, the environment and wildlife as all being intimately interconnected and influenced by the same cosmic forces. Also included here is terminology for the sun, moon and stars, even though, traditionally, they were not considered part of **sila**, but rather of **qilak**, another realm located above **sila** in the sky.*

ᓯᓚ	sila	*weather; environment the outdoors*
ᕿᓚᒃ	qilak	*sky*
ᓯᕿᓂᖅ	siqiniq	*sun*
ᓯᕿᓂᖅ ᓄᐃᔪᖅ	siqiniq nuijuq	*sunrise*
ᓯᕿᓂᖅ ᓂᐱᔪᖅ	siqiniq nipijuq	*sunset*
ᐅᓪᓗᕆᐊᖅ	ulluriaq	*star*
ᑕᖅᑭᖅ	taqqiq	*moon*
ᐊᖅᓴᕐᓃᑦ	aqsarniit	*northern lights*
ᓯᓚ ᖃᓄᐃᑉᐸ?	Sila qanuippa?	*What's the weather like?*
ᓯᕿᓐᓂᖅᑐᖅ	siqinniqtuq	*It's sunny.*
ᓯᓚᑦᑎᐊᕙᒃ	silattiavak	*good weather*
ᓯᓚᖅᑭᖅᑐᖅ	silaqqiqtuq	*clear skies*
ᓄᕗᔭ	nuvuja	*cloud*
ᓄᕗᔭᔪᖅ	nuvujajuq	*It's cloudy.*
ᓂᓪᓚᓱᒃᑐᖅ	nillasuktuq	*cold weather*

ᓯᓚ

ᐅᖅᑰᔪᖅ	uqquujuq	*warm weather*
ᓯᓚᓗᑦᑐᖅ; ᒪᕐᑯᒃᑐᖅ	silaluttuq; makuqtuq	*It's raining.*
ᒥᓂᔪᖅ	minijuq	*It's drizzling.*
ᐊᓄᕆ	anuri	*wind*
ᐊᓄᕌᖅᑐᖅ	anuraaqtuq	*It's windy.*
ᐊᓄᕌᓕᐅᔾᔭᐅᔪᖅ	anuraaliujjaujuq	*caught in heavy winds*
ᐃᑯᓪᓕᐊᖅᑐᖅ	ikulliaqtuq	*There's no wind.*
ᐸᑐᑦᑐᖅ	patuttuq	*There's ice fog.*
ᑕᑦᓯᖅᑐᖅ	tatsiqtuq	*It's foggy.*
ᓂᑦᑕᐃᑦᑐᖅ	nittaittuq	*weather with low visibility*
ᓱᓐᓇᐃᑦᑐᖅ	sunnaittuq	*stormy weather*
ᐊᐳᑦ	aput	*snow*
ᐊᐱᔪᖅ	apijuq	*snow falls (and covers)*
ᐊᐱᓯᒪᔪᖅ	apisimajuq	*snow-covered*
ᖃᓐᓂᖅᑐᖅ	qanniqtuq	*It's snowing.*
ᓇᑎᕈᕕᐊᖅᑐᖅ	natiruviaqtuq	*drifting snow*
ᐱᖅᓯᖅᑐᖅ	piqsiqtuq	*It's blizzarding.*
ᐊᐳᑎᑖᖅᑲᐅᖅ	aputitaaqqauq	*when there has just been a snowstorm*
ᐸᑑᑕᓕᒃ	patuutalik	*light dusting of snow*
ᐳᑲᔮᒃ	pukajaak	*old snow (hard like ice)*
ᑎᓯᓪᓗᖃᖅ	tisilluqaq	*hard packed snow*
ᕿᖅᓱᖅᑲᖓᔪᖅ	qiqsuqqangajuq	*spring snow that softens during the day & freezes at night*
ᒪᙴᒪᔪᖅ	mannguumajuq	*mushy spring snow*
ᓯᑯᕐᓚᒃ	sikurlak	*snow where only the surface is iced up & hard*

environment : weather

ᓄᓇ

land

ᓄᓇ	nuna	*land*
ᐊᐅᔪᐃᑦᑐᖅ	aujuittuq	*glacier*
ᑭᙵᐃᑦ	kinngait	*mountains*
ᖃᖅᑲᖅ	qaqqaq	*mountain*
ᐃᓐᓈᕈᖅ	innaaruq	*cliff*
ᒪᔪᖅᑲᐃᑦ	majuqqait	*steep inclines*
ᖃᖅᑲᔮᖅ	qaqqajaaq	*hill*
ᐳᖅᑐᔪᑦ	puqtujut	*highlands*
ᓇᖅᓴᖅ	naqsaq	*valley*
ᖃᐃᖅᓱᒑᖅ	qaiqsugaaq	*rocky ground*
ᐃᓗᐃᓕᖅ	iluiliq	*mainland*
ᓄᕗᐊ	nuvua	*point*
ᕿᑭᖅᑕᖅ	qikiqtaq	*island*
ᒪᕐᕋᖅ	marraq	*mud on the ground*
ᓯᐅᕋᖅ	siuraq	*sand*
ᑐᐊᐸᒃ	tuapak	*gravel*
ᐅᔭᕋᖅ	ujaraq	*rock*

ᐃᒪᖅ
water

ᐃᒪᖅ	imaq	*an expanse of water*
ᑕᓯᖅ	tasiq	*lake*
ᑕᓯᐊᕐᔪᒃ	tasiarjuk	*pond*
ᑰᒃ	kuuk	*river*
ᑰᒐᓛᒃ	kuugalaak	*creek*
ᖁᓗᕐᓂᖅ	qurlurniq	*waterfall*
ᑕᕆᐅᖅ	tariuq	*sea*
ᐃᑭᖅ	ikiq	*narrow passage; strait*
ᐃᒪᐅᑉ ᓯᓈ	imaup sinaa	*seashore*
ᓯᔾᔭ	sijja	*water's edge (land/ice)*
ᑲᖏᖅᑐᒃ	kangiqtuk	*inlet; fiord*
ᑕᓯᐅᔭᖅ	tasiujaq	*bay*
ᐱᑐᕐᓂᕕᒃ	piturnivik	*tide at full moon*
ᑎᓂᖕᒐᔪᖅ	tiningajuq	*low tide*
ᐅᓕᑦᑐᖅ	ulittuq	*high tide*
ᐃᖏᐅᓕᑦᑐᖅ	ingiulittuq	*large swells*
ᒪᓪᓕᖅᑐᖅ	malliqtuq	*wavy*
ᖃᒑᖅᑐᖅ	qagaaqtuq	*whitecaps*
ᐅᖅᓱᐊᖅᑐᖅ	uqsuaqtuq	*smooth, calm seas*
ᓯᒃᑯ	siku	*ice*

photo: Nunavut Tourism

ᐆᒪᔮᐃᑦ

animals

ᐳᐃᔨ	puiji	*any sea mammal that pops its head out of the water*
ᓇᑦᑎᖅ	nattiq	*ringed seal*
ᓇᑦᑎᕙᒃ	nattivak	*hooded seal*
ᖃᐃᕈᓕᒃ	qairulik	*harp seal*
ᖃᓯᒋᐊᖅ	qasigiaq	*harbour seal*
ᐅᔾᔪᒃ	ujjuk	*bearded seal*
ᐊᐃᕕᖅ	aiviq	*walrus*
ᖀᓚᓗᒐᖅ	qilalugaq	*beluga (also, narwhal in some dialects)*
ᑎᑳᒍᓪᓕᒃ	tikaagullik	*minke whale*
ᑑᒑᓕᒃ	tuugaalik	*narwhal*
ᐊᕐᕕᒃ	arvik	*bowhead whale*
ᐋᕐᓗᒃ	aarluk	*orca; killer whale*

ᐃᑭᕐᒥᐅᑕᐃᑦ	ikirmiutait	*creatures that live in a strait of water*
ᑕᓪᓗᕈᓐᓇᖅ	tallurunnaq	*scallop*
ᐃᖃᓗᒃ	iqaluk	*fish; char*
ᖃᓕᕋᓕᒃ	qaliralik	*turbot*
ᐆᒐᖅ	uugaq	*cod*
ᑎᓂᓂᕐᒥᐅᑕᐃᑦ	tininirmiutait	*creatures of the low tide*
ᑲᓇᔪᖅ	kanajuq	*sculpin*
ᐊᒻᒨᒪᔪᖅ	ammuumajuq	*clam*
ᖁᔾᔭᐅᓐᓇᑦ	qujjaunnat	*eel*
ᑯᐊᓐᓂᖅ	kuanniq	*seaweed (long, fern-like)*
ᐃᖂᑎᑦ	iquutit	*seaweed (frilly)*
ᐅᕕᓗᖅ	uviluq	*mussel*
ᑭᓕᐅᒐᐃᑦ	kiliugait	*barnacles*

land mammals

ᐱᓱᒃᑎᑦ	pisuktit	*land animals*
ᐊᒃᖤᒃ	akłak	*grizzly bear*
ᓇᓄᖅ	nanuq	*polar bear*
ᑐᑦᑐ	tuttu	*caribou*
ᐅᑲᓕᖅ	ukaliq	*rabbit*
ᐅᒥᒻᒪᒃ	umimmak	*musk ox*
ᑎᕆᒐᓂᐊᖅ	tiriganiaq	*arctic fox*
ᐊᒪᕈᖅ	amaruq	*wolf*
ᑎᕆᐊᖅ	tiriaq	*weasel*
ᖃᕝᕕᒃ	qavvik	*wolverine*
ᐊᕕᙳᖅ	avinngaq	*lemming*
ᓯᒃᓯᒃ	siksik	*arctic ground squirrel*

birds

ᓂᒥᐊᑦ	timmiat	*birds*
ᑐᓗᒐᖅ	tulugaq	*raven*
ᐊᒃᐸ	akpa	*murre*
ᐊᕐᕿᒋᖅ	aqiggiq	*ptarmigan*
ᑲᖑᖅ	kanguq	*snow goose*
ᓂᕐᓕᒃ	nirlik	*Canada goose*
ᒥᑎᖅ	mitiq	*duck*
ᓇᐅᔭᖅ	naujaq	*seagull*
ᐅᑉᐱᒃ	uppik	*snowy owl*
ᐃᒥᖅᑯᑕᐃᓚᖅ	imiqqutailaq	*arctic tern*
ᖁᐸᓄᐊᖅ	qupanuaq	*snow bunting*
ᑲᓪᓗᓕᒃ	kallulik	*arctic loon*
ᐱᑦᑎᐅᓛᖅ	pittiulaaq	*black guillemot*
ᒪᓐᓃᑦ	manniit	*eggs*

ᐊᖑᓇᓱᒃᑐᖅ

hunting

ANCIENT SKILLS, MODERN TECHNOLOGY

Hunting remains a fundamental part of the Inuit way of life. Whether on the coast or inland, communities depend on hunting to provide food, clothing and income.

Although snowmobiles, motorboats and all-terrain vehicles are used today, traditional skills and knowledge passed down through generations are essential to hunting in the Arctic environment. In a bid to promote conservation and traditional practices, polar bear hunting is restricted to hunters travelling by dog team or by foot.

ᐊᖑᓇᓱᒃᑐᖅ	angunasuktuq	*hunting*
ᐆᒪᔪᖅᓯᐅᕐᕕᒃ	uumajuqsiurvik	*an area where wildlife is hunted*
ᑐᑦᑐᓯᐅᕐᕕᒃ	tuttusiurvik	*an area where caribou are hunted*
ᐊᓪᓗ	allu	*hole in the ice where seals come up to breathe*
ᐃᓪᓗᐃᓇᖅᑑᑦ	illuinaqtuut	*gun*
ᖁᑭᐅᑦ	qukiut	*rifle*
ᕿᙵᑦ	qinngut	*scope*
ᓴᒃᑯᑦ	sakkut	*bullets*
ᓴᕕᒃ	savik	*knife*
ᑐᒦᑦ	tumiit	*tracks*
ᑐᑦᑐᒧᑦ ᑐᒦᑦ	tuttumut tumiit	*caribou tracks*
ᐊᕿᒡᒋᒧᑦ ᑐᒦᑦ	aqiggimut tumiit	*ptarmigan tracks*
ᑎᕆᒐᓂᐊᒧᑦ ᑐᒦᑦ	tiriganiamut tumiit	*fox tracks*
ᓇᓄᕐᒧᑦ ᑐᒦᑦ	nanurmut tumiit	*bear tracks*

ᐊᒪᕈᕐᒧᑦ ᑐᒦᑦ	amarurmut tumiit	*wolf tracks*
ᑐᑦᑐᒧᑦ ᐊᓇᐃᑦ	tuttumut anait	*caribou droppings*
ᐊᕿᒡᒋᒧᑦ ᐊᓇᐃᑦ	aqiggimut anait	*ptarmigan droppings*
ᐊᒥᖅ	amiq	*skin (land animals)*
ᕿᓯᒃ	qisik	*skin (sea mamals)*
ᐊᐅᒃ	auk	*blood*
ᑭᖑᓪᓖᒃ	kingulliik	*hind leg*
ᑭᐊᓯᒃ	kiasik	*shoulder*
ᑐᓐᓄᖅ	tunnuq	*fat from a land animal*
ᐅᖅᓱᖅ	uqsuq	*fat from a sea mammal*
ᑐᓕᒫᑦ	tulimaat	*ribs*
ᐅᖃᖅ	uqaq	*tongue*
ᐃᔩᒃ	ijiik	*eyes*
ᐃᕙᓗ	ivalu	*sinew*
ᐅᓕᐅᑏᒃ	uliutiik	*tendon*
ᓇᔾᔪᒃ	najjuk	*antler*
ᑐᑦᑐᓕᐊᖅᓯᒪᕙ?	Tuttuliaqsimava?	*Has he gone caribou hunting?*
ᐅᒥᐊᒃᑯᑦ	umiakkut	*by boat*
ᖃᒧᑕᐅᔭᒃᑯᑦ	qamutaujakkut	*by snowmobile*
ᐱᓲᑎᒃᑯᑦ ᑎᓴᒪᓕᒃᑯᑦ	pisuutikkut tisamalikkut	*by four-wheeler*

ᑐᒥᓯᐊᖅᐱᑦ?
tumisiaqpit?
Did you see tracks?

ᖁᑭᖅᐱᐅᒃ?
qukiqpiuk?
Did you hit it?

ᖁᑭᖅᑕᕋ.
qukiqtara
I hit it.

ᐊᓐᓇᐃᔭᕋ.
annaijara
I missed it.

ᑐᑦᑐᓕᐊᖅᑐᖅ
tuttuliaqtuq
He/she is hunting caribou.

ᑐᑦᑐᓂᖅᐸ?
tuttuniqpa?
Did he get a caribou?

ᐄ, ᐊᑕᐅᓯᕐᒥᒃ ᑐᑦᑐᑦᑐᒥᓂᖅ.
ii, atausirmik tuttuttuminiq.
Yes, he got one caribou.

ᑐᑦᑐᑦᑐᖅ
tuttuttuq
He/she caught a caribou.

ᓇᓐᓂᐊᖅᑐᖅ
nanniaqtuq
He/she is hunting polar bear.

ᐅᑲᓪᓕᐊᖅᑐᖅ
ukalliaqtuq
He/she's hunting Arctic hare.

ᐅᑲᓕᖅᑐᖅ
ukaliqtuq
He/she caught a hare.

ᕿᓚᓗᒃᑭᐊᖅᑐᖅ
qilalukkiaqtuq
He/she is hunting whale.

ᕿᓚᓗᒐᖅᑐᖅ
qilalugaqtuq
He/she caught a whale.

ᓇᑦᑎᕋᓱᒋᐊᖅᑐᖅ
nattirasugiaqtuq
He/she is hunting seal.

ᐊᓪᓗᓯᐅᖅᑐᖅ
allusiuqtuq
He looks for seals' breathing holes.

ᒪᐅᓕᖅᑐᖅ
mauliqtuq
He/she hunts seals at their breathing holes.

ᓇᑦᑎᖅᑐᖅ
nattiqtuq
He/she caught a ringed seal.

ᐅᔾᔪᒐᓱᒋᐊᖅᑐᖅ
ujjugasugiaqtuq
He/she is hunting bearded seal.

ᐅᔾᔪᑦᑐᖅ
ujjuttuq
He/she caught a bearded seal.

ᓇᑦᑎᕐᒥᒃ ᐱᓚᑦᑐᖅ
Nattirmik pilattuq.
He/she cuts a ringed seal.

ᐋᑦᑐᖅᑐᖅ
Tuktumik aattuqtuq.
He/she cuts a caribou.

in conversation: **did you go hunting?**

» ᑐᑦᑐᓕᐊᖅᑲᐅᕕᑦ?
Tuttuliaqqauvit?
Did you go caribou hunting?

ᑐᑦᑐᓕᐊᖅᑲᐅᔪᖓ.
Tuttuliaqqaujunga.
I went caribou hunting. «

» ᑭᓱᖅᑲᐅᕕᑦ?
kisuqqauvit?
Did you get anything?

ᐱᖓᓱᓂᒃ ᑐᑦᑐᖅᑲᐅᔪᖓ.
Pingasunik tuttuqqaujunga.
I got three caribou. «

ᐊᑕᐅᓯᕌᖅᑲᐅᔪᖓ.
Atausiraaqqaujunga.
Just one.

ᑭᓱᖅᑲᐅᙱᑦᑐᖓ.
Kisuqqaunngittunga
I didn't get anything.

» ᑐᑦᑐᑦ ᖃᓂᓪᓕᕙᑦ?
Tuttut qanillivat?
Are there caribou close to town?

ᑐᑦᑐᑦ ᖃᓂᓪᓕᔪᑦ.
Tuttut qanillijut.
The caribou are close. «

ᒫᓐᓇ ᑐᑦᑐᑦ ᐅᖓᓯᑦᑐᑦ.
Maanna tuttut ungasittut.
The caribou are far away.

» ᓇᑦᑎᖅᓯᐅᕆᐊᖅᑲᐅᕕᑦ?
Nattiqsiuriaqqauvit?
Did you go seal hunting?

ᓇᑦᑎᕋᓱᒋᐊᖅᑲᐅᔪᖓ.
Nattirasugiaqqaujunga.
I went seal hunting. «

» ᓇᑦᑎᖅᑲᐅᕕᑦ?
Nattiqqauvit?
Did you get any seal?

ᐱᖓᓱᓂᒃ ᓇᑦᑎᖅᑲᐅᔪᖓ.
Pingasunik nattiqqaujunga.
I got three seals. «

» ᓯᓈ ᖃᓂᓪᓕᕙ?
Sinaa qanilliva?
Is the floe edge close?

ᓯᓈ ᖃᓂᓪᓕᔪᖅ.
Sinaa qanillijuq.
The floe edge is close. «

ᓂᕿᑦ

food

ᐱᕈᖅᑐᑦ	piruqtut	*plants*
ᐊᖅᐱᒃ	aqpik	*cloudberry*
ᑭᒍᑕᙱᕐᓇᖅ	kigutangirnaq	*blueberry*
ᑭᒻᒥᓐᓇᖅ	kimminnaq	*cranberry*
ᐸᐅᕐᖓᖅ	paurngaq	*crowberry*
ᖁᖑᓕᑦ	qunguliit	*mountain sorrel*
ᑐᖅᑕᒃ	tuqtak	*bistort*

THE 100 MILE DIET

The Inuit diet reflects the diversity of food that the land and sea provide. What is eaten in each community varies according to what is available locally. Whereas sea mammals are the staple of most Inuit communities, those living away from the coast depend almost entirely on pisuktit *(land animals) for their "country" food.* Akłak *(grizzly bear) is eaten in Baker Lake and other mainland communities, but is unheard of on* Qikiqtaaluk *(Baffin Island) where the only bears are* nanuit *(polar bears).*

uncooked food

ᐅᔪᓰᒪᙱᑦᑐᑦ	uusimanngittut	*uncooked food*
ᐃᒍᓇᖅ	igunaq	*fermented walrus meat*
ᒥᑭᒐᖅ	mikigaq	*raw meat*
ᒥᑭᒐᖅᑐᖅᑐᑦ	mikigaqtuqtut	*feasting on fresh seal*
ᓂᒃᑯᒃ	nikkuk	*dried meat*
ᖁᐊᖅ	quaq	*frozen meat*
ᑭᒃᑲᖅ	kikkaq	*bones with meat*
ᑭᒃᑲᔭᒃᑐᑦ	kikkajaktut	*feasting on fresh caribou*
ᓯᖅᑯᖅ	siqquq	*aged seal flipper*
ᐱᑦᑎ	pitti	*dried fish*
ᒪᑦᑖᖅ	mattaaq	*skin of beluga or narwhal*

cooked food

ᐅᔪᓯᒪᔪᑦ	uusimajut	*cooked food*
ᐊᒡᒍᓛᑕ ᑭᓵᖅ	aggualaqisaaq	*stew*
ᐅᔪᖅ	uujuq	*boiled meat*
ᖃᔪᖅ	qajuq	*broth*
ᐳᓐᓂᕐᓂᖅ	punnirniq	*boiled caribou fat (hardened)*

coffee & tea

ᐃᒥᖅ	imiq	*water for drinking*
ᑲᐱ	kaapi	*coffee*
ᑏ	tii	*tea*
ᓱᑲᖅ	sukaq	*sugar*
ᐃᒻᒧᒃ	immuk	*milk*
ᐸᓚᐅᒑᖅ	palaugaaq	*bannock*
ᓯᕙᐅᔭᖅ	sivaujaq	*cookie*

94

ᐅᐧᓄᒃ ᓂᕿᓕᐅᕆᓂᐊᖅᐱᑦ?
Unnuk niqiliurniaqpit?
Are you cooking tonight?

ᑳᐸᑦ?
kaappit?
Are you hungry?

ᑳᒃᑐᖕᒐ
kaaktunga
I am hungry.

ᑳᓪᓚᕆᓕᖅᑐᖕᒐ
kaallariliqtunga
I'm famished.

ᐊᕿᐊᑦᑐᖅᑐᖕᒐ
aqiattuqtunga
I am full.

ᓂᕆᒌᖅᑲᐅᔪᖕᒐ
nirigiiqqaujunga
I've already eaten.

ᐃᒥᕈᑉᐱᑦ?
imiruppit?
Are you thirsty?

ᓂᕆᒋᑦ
nirigit
Have something to eat.

ᑐᑦᑐᒥᓂᖅᑐᕈᒪᙳᓐᓇᕕᑦ?
tuttuminiqturumannginnavit?
Don't you want any caribou?

ᓇᑦᑎᒥᓂᖅᑐᖓᕈᒪᔪᖕᒐ
nattiminiqtungaarumajunga
I'd rather have some seal.

ᐅᔪᖅᓱᓐᓂᑯᓗᒃ
uujuqsunnikuluk
The uujuq smells delicious.

ᐸᓚᐅᒑᖅᑕᖃᖅᐸ?
palaugaaqtaqaqpa?
Is there any bannock?

ᐸᓚᐅᒑᖅᑐᕆᑦ
palaugaaqturit
Have some bannock.

ᐸᓚᐅᒑᖅᑐᕈᒪᔪᖕᒐ
palaugaaqturumajunga
Give me some bannock.

ᔮᓕᕈᒪᕖᑦ?
jaalirumaviit?
Do you want jam?

ᔮᓕᕈᒪᔪᖕᒐ
jaalirumajunga
I would like jam.

ᒪᑕᓕᕈᒪᔪᖕᒐ
matalirumajunga
I would like butter.

ᐅᓇ ᒪᒪᓪᓚᕆᑦᑐᖅ.
Una mamallarittuq.
This is really good.

ᒪᒪᕆᕕᐅᒃ?
mamariviuk?
Do you like the taste of it?

ᒪᒪᕆᔭᕋ.
mamarijara.
I like the taste of it.

ᐱᒃᑲᓐᓂᕆᑦ
pikkannirit
Have some more.

ᓇᑯᕐᒦᒃ ᓂᕆᑎᒃᑲᕕᙵ.
Nakurmiik niritikkavinnga.
Thank you for the meal.

in conversation: **coffee time**

>> ᖃᐳᑐᕈᒪᕵᑦ?
Kaapiturumaviit?
Would you like coffee?

ᖃᐳᑐᕈᒪᔪᖓ. <<
Kaapiturumajunga.
I would like coffee.

ᖃᐳᑐᕈᒪᙱᑦᑐᖓ.
Kaapiturumanngittunga.
I don't want coffee.

>> ᑎᑐᕈᒪᕵᑦ?
Tiiturumaviit?
Would you like tea?

ᑎᑐᕈᒪᔪᖓ. <<
Tiiturumajunga.
I would like tea.

ᑎᑐᕈᒪᙱᑦᑐᖓ.
Tiiturumanngittunga.
I don't want tea.

>> ᐃᒥᕈᒪᕵᑦ?
Imirumaviit?
Would you like water?

ᐃᒥᕈᒪᔪᖓ. <<
Imirumajunga.
I would like water.

ᐃᒥᕈᒪᙱᑦᑐᖓ.
Imirumanngittunga.
I don't want water.

>> ᓱᑲᓯᓲᖑᕕᑦ?
Sukalisuunguviit?
Do you take sugar?

ᓱᑲᓯᓲᖑᔪᖓ. <<
Sukalisuungujunga.
I take sugar.

ᓱᑲᓯᓲᖑᙱᑦᑐᖓ.
Sukalisuungunngittunga.
I do not take sugar.

>> ᐃᒻᒧᓯᓲᖑᕕᑦ?
Immulisuunguviit?
Do you take milk?

ᐃᒻᒧᓯᓲᖑᔪᖓ. <<
Immulisuungujunga.
I take milk.

photo: Leena Evic

ᐊᐅᑦᓚᖃᕐᓯᒪᕋᖅ

camping

ᑐᐱᖅ	tupiq	tent (modern)
ᐃᑦᑕᖅ	ittaq	traditional skin tent
ᐃᓗᓪᓛᕌᖅ	illuralaaq	cabin
ᑐᐱᕐᕕᒃ	tupirvik	place for pitching tents
ᐱᕈᑦ	pirut	rocks for securing a tent
ᓄᖅᑲᕈᑏᑦ	nuqarutit	ropes for securing a tent
ᓱᐳᐅᔪᖅ	supuujuq	camp stove
ᐅᖅᓱᒃᓴᖅ	uqsuksaq	camp fuel; white gas
ᐆᓇᖅᓯᑎ	uunaqsiti	tea kettle
ᓵᑦᑑᔭᐅᑦ	saattuujaut	frying pan
ᐸᓕᐊᖅ	paliaq	plate
ᐊᓗᑦ	aluut	spoon
ᑲᑭᐊᒃ	kakiak	fork
ᓴᕕᒃ	savik	knife
ᐃᕐᖑᓯᖅ	irngusiq	cup
ᐳᖅ; ᓯᓂᕝᕕᒃ	puuq; sinivvik	sleeping bag
ᐸᑎᐅᔭᖅ	patiujaq	candle
ᐃᑯᒪᑦ	ikumat	matches
ᓈᓚᐅᑦ	naalaut	radio

ᑕᒻᒪᓃᒃᑯᑦ
ᑕᐅᕙᓂ ᐃᓪᓗᕋᓛᖃᖅᑐᒍᑦ
Tauvani illuralaaqaqtugut.
We have a cabin around there.

ᑕᐅᕙᓂ ᑐᐱᖅᓯᒪᔪᖅ.
Tauvani tupiqsimajuq.
She/he has a tent there.

ᐃᓪᓗᕋᓛᖃᖅᑐᖓ ᐃᖃᓗᐃᑦ
ᖃᓂᒋᔮᓂ
illuralaaqaqtunga Iqaluit
qanigijaani
I have a cabin close to Iqaluit.

ᑐᐱᕐᕕᒐ ᐋᓯᕙᓕᐊᓗᒃ
Tupirviga aasivalialuk.
My tent site has many spiders.

ᐃᓪᓗᕋᓛᓕᐊᖅᑕ
illuralaaliaqta
Let's go to the cabin.

ᖃᓄᖅ ᐊᑯᓂᐅᑎᒋᔪᖅ ᑕᐅᕙᓃᓛᖅᐱᑦ?
Qanuq akuniutigijuq tauvaniilaaqpit?
How long are you going to be out there?

ᐃᓪᓗᕋᓛᖅᑕᖃᖅᐸ ᖃᓂᑦᑐᒥ?
Illuralaaqtaqaqpa qanittumi?
Is there a cabin close by?

ᖃᓄᖅ ᐅᖓᓯᑦᑎᒋᕙ ᐃᓪᓗᕋᓛᒧᑦ
Qanuq ungasittigiva illuralaamut?
How far to the cabin?

ᐃᑲᔪᕐᓚᖓ?
ikajurlanga?
Can I help?

ᐱᓇᓱᐊᕈᓯᐅᑉ ᓄᙳᐊᓂ ᑐᐱᕐᒦᓂᐊᖅᐱᑦ?
Pinasuarusiup nunnguani
tupirmiiniaqpit?
Will you be at your tent this weekend?

ᓈᑦᑕᐃᓕᒋᑦ ᓄᖃᕈᑎᓄᑦ!
Naattailigit nuqarutinut!
Careful you don't trip on the nuqarutit!

ᐱᕈᑎᑦ ᒥᑭᔫᑎᐊᓗᐃᑦ
Pirutit mikijuutialuit.
The rocks for anchoring the tent are small.

ᓄᖃᕈᑎᒃᑲ ᑕᑭᔫᑎᑦ
Nuqarutikka takijuutit.
The ropes for anchoring my tent are long.

ᖁᓪᓕᖅ ᐃᑯᒪᕙ?
Qulliq ikumava?
Is the lamp lit?

ᐃᑯᒪᑕᖃᖅᐸ?
Ikumataqaqpa?
Is there a fire going?

ᐆᓇᖅᓯᑏᑦ ᖃᐃᒍᒃ
Uunaqsitiit qaiguk.
Give me the kettle.

ᓵᑦᑑᔭᕐᓂᐊᖅᑐᖓ ᑐᑦᑐᒥᓂᕐᒥᒃ
Saattuujarniaqtunga
tuttuminirmik
I will fry up some caribou meat.

ᐸᓕᐊᑦ ᐅᐊᓴᕆᐊᓖᑦ
Paliat uasarialiit
The plates need to be washed.

ᓴᕕᒃ ᐃᐱᑦᓴᕆᐊᓕᒃ
Savik ipitsarialik.
The knife needs to be sharpened.

ᐴᕐᓂᒃ ᓇᔅᓴᓂᐊᖅᑯᑎᑦ
Puurnik nassaniaqqutit.
Bring the sleeping bags.

in conversation: **Did you go to your cabin?**

» ᐃᓪᓗᕋᓛᓕᐊᓚᐅᖅᐱᑦ?
illuralaalialauqpit?
Did you go to your cabin?

ᐃᓪᓗᕋᓛᓕᐊᓚᐅᖅᑐᖓ
illuralaalialauqtunga
I went to my cabin. «

» ᖃᓄᑎᒋ ᐃᓪᓗᕋᓛᒦᓚᐅᖅᐱᑦ?
Qanutigi illuralaamiilauqpit
How long were you out there?

ᐱᓇᓱᐊᕈᓯᓕᒫᖅ
pinasuarusilimaaq
All week. «

ᐅᓐᓄᐊᖏᓐᓇᖅ
unnuanginnaq
just one night

» ᐅᖓᓯᑉᐸ?
ungasippa?
Is it far?

ᐅᖓᓯᑦᑐᖅ
ungasittuq
It's far. «

ᖃᓂᑦᑐᖅ
qanittuq
It's close.

» ᐃᑲᔪᕈᓐᓇᖅᐱᙵ?
Ikajurunnaqpinnga?
Can you lend me a hand?

ᐃᑲᔪᖅᑕᐅᔪᒪᕕᑦ ᑐᐱᖅᑐᓕᕈᕕᑦ?
Ikajuqtaujumavit tupiqtuliruvit?
Do you need help putting up your tent? «

» ᑐᐲᑦ ᓇᑉᐸᓚᐅᖅᐱᐅᒃ?
Tupiit nappalauqpiuk?
Did you put up your tent?

ᑐᐱᓚᐅᖅᑐᖓ
tupilauqtunga
I put up my tent. «

ᑐᐱᖅᓯᒪᔪᒍᑦ ᑰᑉ ᓴᓂᐊᓂ
Tupiqsimajugut kuup saniani.
We set up our tent beside the river.

ᐊᐅᓚᑦᓯᓂᖅ
travel

photo: Nunavut Tourism

dogs & ski-doos
boating
air travel

photo: Leena Evic

ᐅᒥᐊᒃᑯᑦ

by boat

ᐅᒥᐊᖅ	umiaq	*boat*
ᖃᔭᖅ	qajaq	*kayak*
ᐃᐴᑦ	ipuut	*paddle; oar*
ᐸᐅᑏᒃ	pautiik	*kayak paddle*
ᐅᓈᖅ	unaaq	*harpoon*
ᐊᑦᑐᓈᖅ	attunaaq	*rope*
ᐊᐅᓚᐅᑎᑦ	aulautit	*outboard motor*
ᐅᖅᓱᐊᓗᒃ; ᒑᓯ	uqsualuk; gaasi	*gasoline*
ᑭᓴᐅᑦ	kisaut	*anchor*
ᑭᓴᕐᕕᒃ	kisarvik	*place to anchor*
ᐅᓕᖕᖓᔪᖅ	ulinngajuq	*It's high tide.*
ᑎᓂᖕᖓᔪᖅ	tininngajuq	*It's low tide.*
ᓯᑯ	siku	*ice*
ᑐᓚᑦᑐᖅ	tulattuq	*landing a boat*
ᓵᕕᑦᑐᖅ	saavittuq	*launching a boat*
ᓯᕗᐊ	sivua	*bow*
ᐊᖁᐊ	aqua	*stern*

ᐅᒥᐊᖃᖅᐱᑦ?
umiaqaqpit?
Do you have a boat?

ᐅᒥᐊᑦᑎ?
umialli?
Where's your boat?

ᐅᒥᐊᖅᑐᖅᑐᖅ
umiaqtuqtuq
She is using/riding in a boat.

ᑭᓴᕐᕕᒻᒥ ᑭᓴᖅᓯᒪᔪᑦ.
Kisarvimmi kisaqsimajut.
They are anchored at the break water.

ᐃᑭᒋᑦ
ikigit
Get in.

ᐃᑭᙱᑲᓚᐅᕆᑦ
ikinngikalaurit
Don't get in yet.

ᐊᓂᓕᕆᑦ/ᓂᐅᓕᕆᑦ
Anilirit/niulirit
You can get out.

ᐊᓂᙱᑲᓚᐅᕆᑦ/ᓂᐅᙱᑲᓚᐅᕆᑦ
aninngikalaurit/niunngikalaurit
Don't get out yet.

ᐊᐅᓚᐅᑎᑦ ᐊᐅᓚᔾᔭᓪᓕᑦ/ᐊᐅᓚᔾᔭᒃᑭᑦ.
Aulautit aulajjallit/aulajjakkit.
Start the motor.

ᐊᒧᒍᒃ ᑭᓴᐅᑦ.
Amuguk kisaut.
Haul in the anchor.

ᐊᖁᑲᐃᓐᓇᕆᓪᓕ.
aqukainnarilli
You drive for a bit.

ᐳᑦᑕᖅᑯᑎᖃᖅᐱᓯ?
puttaqqutiqaqpisi?
Do you have floater suits?

ᓇᐅᒃ ᑕᐃᒪ ᐳᑦᑕᖅᑯᑎᑦ?
Nauk taima puttaqqutit?
Where are the floater suits?

ᒪᓪᓕᖅᑐᐊᓗᒃ
malliqtualuk
The waves are high.

ᐊᓄᕆᓗᐊᖅᑐᖅ
anuriluaqtuq
The wind is too strong.

ᐊᐅᓚᓂᖅᑐᓗᐊᖅᑐᖅ
aulaniqtuluaqtuq
The current is too strong.

ᖃᖓ ᐅᓕᓐᓂᐊᖅᐸ?
Qanga ulinniaqpa?
When will it be high tide?

ᖃᖓ ᑎᓂᓐᓂᐊᖅᐸ?
Qanga tininniaqpa?
When will it be low tide?

ᖃᐅᔨᒪᒋᐊᕆᑦ !
qaujimagiarit!
Watch out!

ᖃᐅᔨᒪᒋᐊᕆᑦ , ᐅᔭᕋᑦᑕᖃᖅᒪᑦ.
Qaujimagiarit, ujarattaqarmat.
Watch, there's a rock.

ᓇᙱᐊᖅᑐᖕᒐ ᐅᒥᐊᖅᑐᕆᐊᔅᓴᖅ.
Nangiaqtunga umiaqturiassaq.
I am afraid of being in the boat.

ᒑᓯᑖᕆᐊᖃᖅᑐᒍᑦ
gaasitaariaqaqtugut
We need to buy gas.

in conversation: **on a boat**

>> ᐃᑭᓚᖕᓚ?
Ikilanga?
Should I get in?

ᐃᑭᒋᑦ <<
ikigit
Get in.

ᐃᑭᑦᑕᕐᓇᒃ
ikittarnak
Don't get in.

ᒫᓐᓇᐅᖕᒋᑦᑐᖅ
maannaungittuq
not now

>> ᓂᐅᓚᖕᓚ?
Niulanga?
Should I get out?

ᓂᐅᒋᑦ <<
niugit
You can get out.

>> ᓂᐅᑦᑕᕐᓇᒃ <<
niuttarnak
Don't get out.

>> ᐃᓚᐅᔪᓐᓇᖅᐳᖕᓚ?
ilaujunnaqpunga?
Can I come along?

ᐃᓚᐅᔪᓐᓇᖅᑐᑎᑦ <<
ilaujunnaqtutit
You can come along.

>> ᓱᓕᖅᐸ?
suliqpa?
What's wrong with it?

ᐊᐅᓚᐅᑎᑦ ᓄᖅᑲᑲᐃᓐᓇᖅᑐᑦ. <<
Aulautit nuqqakainnaqtut.
The motor stopped for a bit.

ᓱᕋᑦᑐᖅ
surattuq
It's broken.

ᒑᓰᕈᑎᔪᒍᑦ
gaasiirutijugut
We ran out of gas.

ᖃᒧᔅᓯᖅᑯᑦ ᖃᒧᑕᐅᔭᖅᑯᑦᓄ

by dog   team   &   ski-doo

ᖃᐃᒻᒥᖅ	qimmiq	*dog*
ᖃᒧᔅᓯᑦ	qimussit	*dog team*
ᐃᐱᐅᑕᑦ	ipiutat	*traces (connect harness to qamutiik)*
ᐊᓄ	anu	*dog harness*
ᐃᐸᕋᐅᑦ	iparaut	*dog whip*
ᐃᓯᕋᖅᑐᔪᖅ	isuraqtujuq	*lead dog*
ᖃᒧᑕᐅᔭᖅ	qamutaujaq	*snowmobile*
ᐸᐃᒡᒑᓚ	paiggaala	*gas can*
ᐅᖅᓱᖅᑎᕈᑦ	uqsuqtirut	*oil*
ᓯᐊᕐᕆᔭᐅᑏᒃ	siarrijautiik	*snowmobile skis*
ᖃᒧᑏᒃ	qamutiik	*sledge; kamotik*
ᐱᕐᕌᒃ	pirraak	*qamutiik runner*
ᑲᓗᑎ	kaluti	*hitch*
ᓇᐳ	napu	*wooden cross-bar (on a qamutiik)*
ᐊᑦᑐᓈᖅ	attunaaq	*rope*
ᐃᑭᒋᑦ	ikigit	*Get on.*
ᓂᐅᒋᑦ	niugit	*Get off.*
ᐅᖓᓯᑉᐹ?	ungasippaa?	*Is it far?*
ᐅᖓᓯᑦᑐᖅ	ungasittuq	*It's far.*
ᖃᓂᑦᑐᕈᓗᒃ	qanitturuluk	*It's close.*
ᖃᐃᖅᐸᓂᒃᑯᔪᖕᒐ; ᖁᐊᕐᓂᖃᖅᑐᖕᒐ	qiqinnikuujunga; quarniqaqtunga	*I have frostbite.*
ᖁᐊᖅᑐᖅ	quaqtuq	*It is frozen.*

travel : dogs & ski-doos

105

ᕿᒧᔅᓯᒃᑯᑦ ᐊᐅᓪᓚᖅᑲᐅᔪᖅ.
Qimussikkut aullaqqaujuq.
She went out by dog team.

ᖃᓂᓪᓕᓗᐊᖅᑕᐃᓕᒋᑦ
qanilliluaqtailigit
Don't go near them.

ᑮᓯᓲᕌᓗᐃᑦ
kiisisuuraaluit
They bite.

ᐃᓱᕋᖅᑐᔪᕐᑯᑏᑦ ᓇᒦᒻᒪᑦ?
Isuraqtujuqutiit namiimmat?
Where is your lead dog?

ᐃᐱᐅᑕᖏᑦ ᓂᒐᕖᔭᒃᑭᑦ.
Ipiutangit nigaviijakkit.
Untangle the traces.

ᐃᐱᐅᑕᖏᑦ ᐃᓪᓚᐃᒃᑭᑦ
ipiutangit illaikkit
Get the traces ready.

ᕿᒻᒦᑦ ᐊᓄᒃᑭᑦ
Qimmiit anukkit
Harness the dogs.

ᐃᑭᒪᑐᐃᓐᓇᕆᑦ
ikimatuinnarit
Stay seated.

ᑲᑕᒐᐅᑦᑕᐃᓕᒋᑦ
katagauttailigit!
Don't fall off!

ᐅᓪᓚᓵᕆᑦ
ullasaarit
Run fast!

ᓇᔪᒻᒥᑐᐃᓐᓇᕆᑦ
najummituinnarit
Hold on tight.

ᐅᓇ ᑎᒍᒥᐊᕈᒃ.
Una tigumiaruk.
Please hold this.

ᑕᖃᕕᑦ?
taqavit?
Are you tired?

ᑕᖃᔪᖓ
taqajunga
I am tired.

ᖃᒧᑕᐅᔭᒃᑯᑦ ᐊᐅᓪᓚᖅᑲᐅᔪᖅ.
Qamutaujakkut aullaqqaujuq.
He went out by ski-doo.

ᒑᓯᑖᕆᐊᖃᖅᑐᖓ
gaasitaariaqaqtunga
I need to buy gas.

ᐅᖅᓱᖅᑎᕈᒻᒥᓪᓗ
uqsuqtirummillu
I also need oil.

ᐅᖅᓱᖅᑎᕈᑕᐃᕈᑎᔪᖓ
uqsuqtirutairutijunga
I'm out of oil.

ᐊᓗᖓ ᓱᕋᔅᓯᒪᔪᖅ.
Alunga surassimajuq.
The track is broken.

ᓯᐊᕐᕆᔭᐅᑎᒪ ᐊᐃᑉᐸᖓ ᓱᕋᒃᓯᒪᔪᖅ?
Siarrijautima aippanga
suraksimajuq.
One of my skis is broken.

ᓇᐳᒃᑲ ᖃᓱᔪᑦ
Napukka qasujut.
My cross bars are loose.

ᐊᑦᑐᓈᖃᖅᐱᑦ?
attunaaqaqpit?
Do you have a rope?

in conversation: **snowmobiling**

>> ᖃᒧᑕᐅᔮᓐᓂᒃ
ᐊᑐᕈᓐᓇᖅᐳᖓ ᒃ?
Qamutaujaannik
aturunnaqpunga .?
*Can I borrow a
snowmobile?*

ᖃᒧᑕᐅᔭᖃᖅᑐᖓ. <<
Qamutaujaqaqtunga.
I have a snowmobile.

>> ᖃᓄᐃᒃᑲᕕᑦ?
Qanuikkavit?
What's wrong?

ᐅᖅᓱᐃᖅᓯᒪᔪᖓ. <<
Uqsuiqsimajunga.
I'm out of gas.

ᑲᓗᑎᒐ ᓱᕋᓯᒪᔪᖅ.
Kalutiga surassimajuq.
The hitch is broken.

ᓯᐊᕆᓐᔭᐅᑎᓪᓕᓯᒪᔪᖓ.
Siarrijautiillisimajunga.
My ski is broken.

ᐊᐅᓚᔾᔭᑯᓐᓇᖏᑦᑐᖅ.
Aulajjagunnangittuq.
It won't start.

>> ᖅᐱᐅᕕᑦ?
Qiuvit?
Are you cold?

ᖃᓄᐃᙱᑦᑐᖓ. <<
Qanuinngittunga.
I'm fine.

ᖅᐱᐅᔪᖓ.
Qiujunga.
I'm cold.

>> ᑲᒪᒋᙱᑲᐃᓐᓇᓕᕆᒃ.
Kamaginngikainnaliruk.
Leave it for a while.

ᐆᒃᑐᓚᐅᕐᒥᒍᒃ. <<
Uuktulaurmiguk.
Try it again.

>> ᑎᐃᓕᐅᕐᓗᓄᒃ.
Tiiliurlunuk.
We'll make some tea.

ᑎᑐᓚᐅᕐᓗᒃ.
Tiitulaurluk.
Let's have some tea.

ᖃᖏᓚᑕᒃᑯᑦ

by air

ᖃᖏᓚᑕᒃ	qangatasuuq	*airplane*
ᖃᖏᓚᑕᒃᑎ	qangatasuuqti	*pilot*
ᖃᖏᓚᑕᒃᑯᕕᒃ	qangatasuukkuvik	*airport; terminal*
ᒥᕝᕕᒃ	mivvik	*landing strip; airstrip*
ᖃᖏᓚᑕᐅᑦ	qangattaut	*ticket*
ᐊᑭᖓ	akinga	*cost*
ᐊᑭᓕᖅᑐᖅ	akiliqtuq	*paid*
ᐸᕐᓇᑦᑐᖅ	parnattuq	*preparing to go*
ᐳᖅᑲᐃᔪᖅ	puuqqaijuq	*packing*
ᐃᑦᑏᕝᕕᒃ	ittirvik	*luggage*
ᐱᔨᑲᑖᑦ	pijikataat	*in-flight crew*
ᐃᑭᓗᓂ	ikiluni	*boarding*
ᐊᑯᓂ	akuni	*long trip*
ᕿᓚᒥ	qilami	*short trip*
ᐊᐅᓪᓚᓕᖅᑐᖅ	aullaliqtuq	*It's departing now.*
ᑎᑭᓕᖅᑐᖅ	tikiliqtuq	*It's arriving now.*
ᒥᑦᑐᖅ	mittuq	*It lands.*

ᐊᐃᑉᐸᑕᖅ : ᖃᖏᓚᑕᒃᑯᑦ

ᖃᖕᒥᑦᑎᓱᖅ ᓇᖕᐁᐊᕐᓇᖅᑐᐊᓗᖅᖃᐅᔪᖅ.
Qangatasuuq
nangiarnaqtualuuqqaujuq.
The flight was pretty scary.

ᓱᓇᕐᕙᓗᖕᒋᓐᓇ?
sunarvalunginna?
What is that noise?

ᒥᕝᕙᓗᑦᑐᖅ
mivvaluttuq
Sounds like it's landed.

ᐃᒡᓗᓕᒻᒧᓛᖅᑐᖕᓇ
iglulimmuulaaqtunga
I'm going to Iglulik.

ᐃᒡᓗᓕᒻᒦᖕᖓᖅᑐᖕᓇ
iglulimmiinngaaqtunga
I'm coming from Iglulik.

ᖃᖕᒥᑦᑎᓱᖅ ᐊᐅᓪᓚᓕᖅᑐᖅ.
Qangatasuuq aullaliqtuq.
The plane is leaving.

ᖃᖕᒥᑦᑎᓱᖅ ᓄᖅᖃᖅᑎᑕᖅ.
Qangatasuuq nuqqaqtitaq.
The flight is cancelled.

ᖃᖕᒥᑦᑎᓱᖅ ᑭᖑᕙᕆᐊᖅᑕᐅᓯᒪᔪᖅ.
Qangatasuuq kinguvariaqtausimajuq.
The flight is delayed.

ᐱᖅᓰᕐᓂᖕᓄᑦ
piqsirninganut
because there is a blizzard

ᐊᓄᕌᖅᑐᐊᓘᒻᒪᑦ
anuraaqtualuummat
because it is too windy.

ᐊᐅᓚᐅᑎᖕᒡᒎᖅ ᖃᖕᒥᑦᑎᓱᑉ
ᐱᐅᖕᒋᒻᒪᑕ.
Aulautingigguuq qangatasuup
piunngimmata.
*because the plane broke down;
went mechanical.*

ᖃᖕᒥᑦᑎᓱᖅ ᑕᑕᑦᑐᖅ/ᐃᓂᖃᖕᒋᑦᑐᖅ.
Qangatasuuq tatattuq/iniqangittuq.
The plane is full.

ᓇᐅᒡᓕ ᐃᑦᑎᕐᕕᒃᑲ?
Naugli ittirvikka?
Where are my bags?

ᓇᓂᔪᓐᓇᖕᖏᑕᒃᑲ ᐃᑦᑎᕐᕕᒃᑲ.
Nanijunnanngitakka ittirvikka.
I can't find my bags.

ᐃᑦᑎᕐᕖᑦ ᐅᖁᒪᐃᑦᑐᐊᓗᒃ.
Ittirviit uqumaittualuk.
Your luggage is heavy.

ᖃᓄᓪᕆ ᓄᓇᓕᓐᓅᓂᐊᖅᐳᖕᓇ?
Qanurli nunalinnuuniaqpunga?
How do I get to town from here?

ᐃᑭᕕᒋᔪᓐᓇᖅᐸᒋᑦ?
ikivigijunnaqpagit?
Can you give me a ride?

ᐃᑭᔪᒪᕕᑦ?
ikijumavit?
Would you like a ride?

ᐱᖃᑏᒪ ᐊᐃᓂᐊᖅᑖᖕᒑ.
Piqatima ainiaqtaanga.
My friend will pick me up.

ᐊᑐᕚᒧᑦ ᐱᖕᖑᐊᕆᐊᖅᑐᓚᐅᖅᑐᖕᓇ
Aatuvaamut pinnguariaqtulauqtunga
*I went to Ottawa to compete in
a sport.*

ᖁᓗᖅᑐᖅᒧᑦ ᐱᖃᑎᒐ
ᑕᑯᔭᖅᑐᓚᐅᖅᑕᕋ.
Qurluqturmut piqatiga
takujaqtulauqtara.
*I went to Kugluktuk to visit my
friend.*

ᐊᑯᑭᑦᑐᓄᑦ ᖁᑭᓂᐊᓚᐅᖅᑐᖕᓇ.
Akukittunut qikarialauqtunga.
I went to Greenland for a holiday.

in conversation: **travel plans**

ᐱᓇᓱᐊᕈᓯᐅᓛᖅᑐᒧᑦ
ᐸᕐᓇᑦᑐᖓ. «
pinasuarusiulaaqtumut
parnattunga.
I plan to go away next week.

»ᓇᒧᑦ ᐸᕐᓇᑉᐱᑦ?
Namut parnappit?
Where do you plan to go?

ᒫᑐᓕᐊᒧᑦ ᐸᕐᓇᑦᑐᖓ. «
Maatuliamut parnattunga.
I plan to go to Montreal.

»ᖃᖓᑦᑕᐅᑏᑦ
ᖃᑦᑎᕌᓚᐅᖅᐸ?
Qangattautiit
qattiraalauqpa?
*How much was your
airplane ticket?*

ᖃᖓᑦᑕᐅᑎᒐ ᐊᕆᖃᓚᐅᖅᑐᖅ
$1,200-ᓂᒃ. «
Qangattautiga akiqalauqtuq
$1,200-nik.
My airplane ticket cost $1,200.

»ᐃᑦᑎᕐᕕᖏᑦ ᖃᑦᑎᐅᓛᖅᐸᑦ?
Ittirvitit qattiulaaqpat?
*How many suitcases will
you have?*

ᑎᓯᒪᓂᒃ ᐃᑦᑎᕐᕕᒋᕐᓂᐅᓴᔪᖓ.
Tisamanik «
ittirviggirniusajunga.
I am bringing four suitcases.

»ᖃᖓᑕᓲᒃᑯᑦ
ᓇᓕᐊᒃᑯᓛᖅᐱᑦ?
Qangatasuukkut
naliakkuulaaqpit?
*Which airline are you
taking?*

ᐳᔅ ᐃᐊᒃᑰᓛᖅᑐᖓ. «
Puus iakkuulaaqtunga.
I am taking First Air.

ᑲᓇᐃᑎᐊᒃᑰᖅᑐᖓ.
Kanaitiakkuuqtunga.
I am taking Canadian North.

»ᐋᑯᓂᐊᓗᒃ
ᐊᐅᓪᓚᖅᓯᒪᓛᖅᐱᑦ?
Aakunialuk
aullaqsimalaaqpit?
*So will you be away very
long?*

ᕿᓚᒥᕈᓗᒃ ᐊᐅᓪᓚᖅᓯᒪᓛᖅᑐᖓ
Qilamiruluk «
aullaqsimalaaqtunga.
*I will be gone for a short
time.*

ᐃᓄᒃᑎᑐᑦ
ᐊᕐᖄᕆᐅᒪᓂᖅ

inuktitut grammar

inuktitut verbs

THE SUBJECT

In Inuktitut, we indicate who we are talking about by using an affix that appears (usually) at the very end of the word:

niri**junga**   *I eat*

Here is a list of the verb endings that indicate who the subject is:

niri**junga**	*I eat*
niri**jutit**	*you eat*
niri**juq**	*he / she eats*
niri**juguk**	*the two of us eat*
niri**jugut**	*we (3 or more) eat*
niri**jusik**	*you two eat*
niri**jusi**	*you (three or more) eat*
niri**juuk**	*the two of them eat*
niri**jut**	*they (three or more) eat*

To make pronunciation easier, the first letter of all of these affixes changes from **j** to **t** when they are added to a root that ends in a consonant.

isiq**tuq**   *he enters*

THE NEGATIVE

In Inuktitut, to express the negative, we often insert the affix **–nngit** just before the subject of the verb:

taqa + **nngit** + tunga = taqa**nngit**tunga   *I am not tired.*

When **-nngit** is added to a root that ends in a consonant, it deletes the final consonant:

quviasuk + nngit + tuq = quviasu**nngit**tuq   *He is not happy.*

ASKING QUESTIONS

To ask a question in Inuktitut we add an affix to the end of a verb. The affix that is used changes depending on who is the subject of the verb:

niri**vit**?	*Are you eating?*
niri**va**?	*Is he eating?*

To make pronunciation easier, the affixes that are used to ask questions change, depending on the last letter of the root to which they are added.

When dealing with roots that end in a **vowel** you add a question affix that begins with the letter **v**:

ani**vunga**?	*Am I leaving?*
ani**vit**?	*Are you leaving?*
ani**va**?	*Is he/she leaving?*
ani**vinuk**?	*Are the two of us leaving?*
ani**vita**?	*Are we (3 or more) leaving?*
ani**visik**?	*Are you two leaving?*
ani**visi**?	*Are you (3 or more) leaving?*
ani**vaak**?	*Are the two of them leaving?*
ani**vat**?	*Are they (3or more) leaving?*

If you want to ask a question with a verb ending in **q**, you use the same endings as above, replacing the **v** with a **p**.

isiq**punga**?	*Am I coming in?*
isiq**pit**?	*Are you coming in?*
isiq**pa**?	*Is he/she coming in?*
isiq**pita**?	*Are we (3 or more) coming in?*
isiq**pisi**?	*Are you (3 or more) coming in?*
isiq**paak**?	*Are the two of them coming in?*
isiq**pat**?	*Are they (3 +) leaving?*

If the verb ends in any other consonant, you do the following:

> * replace the final consonant of the verb with a **p**
> * use the same endings above, replacing the **v** with a **p**.

sinip**punga**?	*Am I sleeping?*
sinip**pit**?	*Are you sleeping?*
sinip**pa**?	*Is he/she sleeping?*
sinip**pinuk**?	*Are the two of us sleeping?*
sinip**pita**?	*Are we (3 or more) sleeping?*
sinip**pisik**?	*Are you two sleeping?*
sinip**pisi**?	*Are you (3 +) sleeping?*
sinip**paak**?	*Are the two of them sleeping?*
sinip**pat**?	*Are they (3 +) sleeping?*

OBJECT OF THE VERB

Consider the following two sentences:

> *I see.*   *I see her.*

The first sentence involves just one person, the subject, or the person who does the seeing. The second sentence involves two people, the subject and an object, or the person who is seen.

Whereas an English speaker would indicate the object using a pronoun, in this case *her,* an Inuktitut speaker would use an affix that indicates both the subject and the object of the sentence at the same time:

taku**junga**	*I see.*
taku**jara**	*I see **her**.*
tusaa**juq**	*She hears.*
tusaa**jaatit**	*She hears **you**.*
malik**tunga**	*I follow.*
malik**takka**	*I follow **them**.*

Here is an expanded (but incomplete) list of these affixes:

	me	you	him / her / it
I		taku**jagit** *I see you.*	taku**jara** *I see him.*
you	taku**jarma** *You see me.*		taku**jait** *You see him.*
he/she	taku**jaanga** *She sees me.*	taku**jaatit** *She sees you.*	taku**janga** *She sees him.*

	me	you	him / her / it
I		taku**jatsi** *I see all of you.*	taku**jakka** *I see all of them.*
you	taku**jattigut** *You see all of us.*		taku**jatit** *You see all of them.*
he/she	taku**jaatigut** *She sees all of us.*	taku**jaasi** *He sees all of you.*	taku**jangit** *She sees all of them.*

Remember that if these affixes are added to roots that end in a consonant, the first letter of the affix changes to **t**:

malik**tara**   *I am following him.*

For asking questions, there is a corresponding set of affixes that involve a direct object. Here are the simplest of them:

	me	you	him / her
I		qaujima**vagit**? *Do I know you?*	qaujima**vara**? *Do I know her?*
you	tusaa**vinga**? *Do you hear me?*		tusaa**viuk**? *Do you hear him?*
he/she	tusaa**vaanga**? *Does she hear me?*	tusaa**vaatit**? *Does she hear you?*	tusaa**vauk**? *Does she hear him?*

THE IMPERATIVE

The imperative is used to tell someone to do something, or indicate something that you would like to happen.

-git is used when you are speaking to one other person:

| niri**git** | *Eat!* |
| qai**git** | *Come here!* |

If **-git** is added to a root ending in a **q**, the **q** is dropped and the affix **-rit** is used:

| uqalimaa**rit** | *Read!* |
| uti**rit** | *Come back!* |

When telling someone to do something, there is often an object involved. In which, case we use different endings:

Tuni**guk** Mialimut   *Take it to Mary!*

Utiqti**guk** kuuqarvimmut   *Take it back to the kitchen!*

THE PAST TENSE

Affixes are used in Inuktitut when we want to indicate that an event has happened in the past. The affix that is used depends on how long ago an event has happened.

-rataaq is an affix that is used to describe actions that have happened in the immediate past (within the hour).

| isi**rataaq**tuq | *She just came in.* |
| tiki**rataaq**tugut | *We just arrived.* |

-qqau is an affix that is used to describe actions that have happened earlier in the day.

| Uqaala**qqau**juq. | *He called earlier.* |
| Angirra**qqau**junga. | *I went home (earlier today).* |

-lauq is used to describe actions that have happened yesterday or in the not too distant past.

Ippassaq tuktulia**lauq**tuq.

Yesterday, he went caribou hunting.

For events further in the past, or if you are vague about when something happened, the affix **-lauqsima** is used:

Aatuvaamiutau**lauqsima**junga.   *I used to live in Ottawa.*

Iglulimmi**lauqsima**viit?   *Have you ever been to Iglulik?*

Note that when any of the above affixes are added to a root ending in a consonant, they delete the final consonant.

THE FUTURE TENSE

One way of forming the future tense in Inuktitut, is to insert the affix **-niaq** between the verb and the subject of the sentence:

Suvit?	*What are you doing?*
Su**niaq**pit?	*What will you be doing?*
nirijunga	*I am eating*
niri**niaq**tunga	*I will be eating*

When **-niaq** is added to a verb stem that ends in **q,** the **q** changes to **r.**

kaapituq + niaq + tunga =

kaapitur**niaq**tunga.

I will be drinking coffee.

When **-niaq** is added to a stem ending in **t** it changes the final **t** to **n.**

tavvaniit + niaq + tuq =

tavvaniin**niaq**tuq

He is going to be here.

In Iqaluit, **-langa** is the affix that is most commonly used for an event in the immediate future:

Ullumi aulla**langa**juq   *He is leaving town today.*

-laaq is another affix that is used to talk about the future. Whereas **-niaq** describes something that will happen in the very near future, **-laaq** is a little farther ahead in time.

aullar**niaq**tunga	*I am departing (later that day).*
aulla**laaq**tunga	*I will be departing (sometime in the future).*
taku**niaq**pugut	*See you soon*
taku**laar**ivugut	*See you later/ See you then.*

If **-laaq** is added to a stem that ends in a consonant, it deletes the last consonant.

nouns

THE DUAL

In English, when we want to talk about more than one of something, we usually add an **s** to the end of a noun:

one door	*two door**s***	*three door**s***

In Inuktitut, we use different endings to distinguish between **two of something** and **more than two** of something:

ulu	*one knife*
ulu**uk**	*(two) knives*
ulu**it**	*(three) knives*

The dual form is used to talk about two of a particular object. You can recognize the dual form as any noun that ends in a double vowel, followed by a **k**.

s**aak**	*(two) tables*
uqaalaut**iik**	*(two) telephones*
ill**uuk**	*(two) houses*

Here's some instructions on changing a noun from its singular form to the dual:

* if the object ends in a **vowel,** double the last vowel and add **k**:

nuvuja	*cloud*
nuvuj**aak**	*(two) clouds*

* if the object ends in a **t**, add the ending **iik**:

paippaamuurijjut	*printer*
paippaamuurijjut**iik**	*(two) printers*

* if it ends in any consonant other than **t**, delete the last consonant, double the last vowel, and add **k**:

kamik	*skin boot*
kam**iik**	*(two) skin boots*

Remember that in Inuktitut, you almost never put together more than two vowels in a row. So if you drop the final consonant and find you already have two vowels, just add **k**:

luuktaaq	*doctor*
luukt**aak**	*(two) doctors*
nunannguaq	*map*
nunanng**uak**	*(two) maps*

THE PLURAL

In Inuktitut, the plural is used to talk about **more than two** of any noun:

inuk	*person*
inuit	*people (3+)*

The plural form always ends in **t**. Here are some instructions on changing a noun from its singular form to the plural:

if the noun ends in a vowel, add **-it**:

ilisaiji	*teacher*
ilisaiji**it**	*teachers (3+)*

If the noun ends in **t**, add **-iit**:

uqaalaut	*telephone*
uqaalaut**iit**	*telephones (3+)*

If the object ends in any other consonant, **delete** the last consonant, and add **-it**:

iqaluk	*fish*
iqalu**it**	*fish (3+)*

If you delete the last consonant, and find that you already have two vowels, just add **t**:

puuq	*bag*
puu**t**	*bags (3+)*

ᑐᑮᑦ

ᐃᓄᒃᑎᑐᑦ - ᖃᑦᓗᓈᑎᑐᑦ

mini-dictionary: inuktitut-english

A

aagga ᐋᒡᒐ *no (S. Baffin)*

aagga suli ᐋᒡᒐ ᓱᓕ *not yet*

aaggiisi ᐋᒡᒌᓯ *August*

aakka ᐋᒃᑲ *no (N. Baffin)*

aamai ᐋᒪᐃ
I don't know (N. Baffin)

aanniaviit? ᐋᓐᓂᐊᕖᑦ?
Are you in pain?

aanniavik ᐋᓐᓂᐊᕕᒃ
hospital / nursing station

aatsuu ᐋᑦᓲ *I don't know (S. Baffin)*

Aatuvaamiutaq ᐋᑐᕚᒥᐅᑕᖅ
He's from Ottawa /
He lives in Ottawa.

aggaak ᐊᒡᒑᒃ *gloves*

aggaak illugiik ᐊᒡᒑᒃ ᐃᓪᓗᒌᒃ
a pair of gloves

aggaak illugiinngittuuk
ᐊᒡᒑᒃ ᐃᓪᓗᒌᙱᑦᑑᒃ
two gloves that don't match

aggaaq illuinnaq ᐊᒡᒑᖅ ᐃᓪᓗᐃᓐᓇᖅ
a single glove

aggak ᐊᒡᒐᒃ *hand*

aggammik ᐊᒡᒐᒻᒥᒃ *ring*

aggaut ᐊᒡᒐᐅᑦ *forearm*

aggualaqisaaq ᐊᒡᒍᐊᓚᕿᓵᖅ
stew

ainiaqtara ᐊᐃᓂᐊᖅᑕᕋ
I will pick her up later.

aippaq ᐊᐃᑉᐸᖅ
partner / common-law

aippiq ᐊᐃᑉᐱᖅ *Tuesday*

Aivilik ᐊᐃᕕᓕᒃ
coast between Chesterfield Inlet
and Repulse Bay

aiviq ᐊᐃᕕᖅ *walrus*

ajjigiik ᐊᔾᔨᒌᒃ *They are the same.*

ajjigiinngittuuk ᐊᔾᔨᒌᙱᑦᑑᒃ
They are different.

akaugijara ᐊᑲᐅᒋᔭᕋ
I like her / him / it

akautsianngittunga
ᐊᑲᐅᑦᓯᐊᙱᑦᑐᖓ
I don't feel well.

akianiittuq ᐊᑭᐊᓃᑦᑐᖅ
it's on the other side

akikittuq ᐊᑭᑭᑦᑐᖅ *cheap*

akilissaq ᐊᑭᓕᔅᓴᖅ *the bill*

akinga ᐊᑭᖓ *price / cost*

mini-dictionary : inuktitut - english

akitujuq ⊲ᑭᑐᓴᖅ   *expensive*

akłak ⊲ᖅᓚᒃ   *grizzly bear*

akpa ⊲ᑉ<   *murre*

Akukittuq ⊲ᑯᑭᑦᑐᖅ   *Greenland*

akunninganiittuq ⊲ᑯᓐᓂᖓᓂᐅᑦᑐᖅ
   it's between

akuq ⊲ᑯᖅ *amauti (long tailed)*

alianait ⊲ᓕᐊᓇᐃᑦ   *It's wonderful.*

allavvik ⊲ᓪᓚᕝᕕᒃ   *office*

allirujaak ⊲ᓪᓕᕈᔮᒃ   *scissors*

allu ⊲ᓪᓗ
   hole in the ice where seals come
   up to breathe

allusiuqtuq ⊲ᓪᓗᓯᐅᖅᑐᖅ
   He looks for seals' breathing holes.

aluut ⊲ᓘᑦ   *spoon*

amaruq ⊲ᒪᕈᖅ   *wolf*

amarurmut tumiit ⊲ᒪᕐᒧᑦ ᑐᒦᑦ
   wolf tracks

amauti ⊲ᒪᐅᑎ
   parka with pouch at the back for
   carrying a child

amiat ⊲ᒥⰀᑦ   *colours*

amiq ⊲ᒥᖅ   *skin (land animals)*

amisuliurut ⊲ᒥᓱᓕᐅᕈᑦ
   photocopier

amisut ⊲ᒥᓱᑦ   *lots / many*

amisuunngittut ⊲ᒥᓲᖕᒋᑦᑐᑦ
   few /not many

ammalu ⊲ᒻᒪᓗ   *and*

ammuumajuq ⊲ᒻᒨᒪᔪᖅ
   clam

anaana ⊲ᓈᓇ   *mother*

anaanatsiaq ⊲ᓈᓇᑦᓯⰀᖅ
   grandmother

anarvik ⊲ᓇᕐᕕᒃ   *washroom*

anaullagat ⊲ᓇᐅᓪⰇᒏᑦ
   drums

angijuk ⊲ᖕᒋᔪᒃ
   older sibling (of same sex)

angijuq ⊲ᖕᒋᔪᖅ   *big*

angijuqtaq ⊲ᖕᒋᔪᖅᑕᖅ
   skirt

angijuqtaujaq ⊲ᖕᒋᔪᖅᑕᐅᔭᖅ
   amauti (skirted style)

angiluaqtuq ⊲ᖕᒋᓗⰀᖅᑐᖅ
   It is too big.

angirraliqtunga ⊲ᖕᒋᕐᕋᓕᖅᑐᖕⰇ
   I am on my way home.

angunasuktuq ⊲ᖑᓇᓱᒃᑐᖅ
   hunting

anijuq ⊲ᓂᔪᖅ   *He/she leaves.*

anik ⊲ᓂᒃ
   brother of a female

anikainnaqsimajuq
   ⊲ᓂᑲᐃᓐᓇᖅᓯᒪᔪᖅ.
   He/she has stepped out.

annuraaqtuq ⊲ᓐᓄⰓᖅᑐᖅ
   He/she gets dressed.

annuraat ⊲ᓐᓄⰓᑦ   *clothing*

anu ⊲ᓄ   *dog harness*

anuraaliujjaujuq ⊲ᓄⰓᓕᐅᔾᔭᐅᔪᖅ
   caught in heavy winds

anuraaqtuq ⊲ᓄⰓᖅᑐᖅ   *It's windy.*

anuri ⊲ᓄᕆ   *wind*

apijuq ⊲ᐱᔪᖅ
   becomes covered with snow

apisimajuq ⊲ᐱᓯᒪᔪᖅ *snow-covered*

aput ᐊᐳᑦ *snow*

aputitaaqqauq ᐊᐳᑎᑖᖅᑲᐅᖅ
when there has just been a
snowstorm

aqiattuqtunga ᐊᖅᐊᑦᑐᖅᑐᖕᒐ
I am full.

aqiggimut anait ᐊᖅᐱᕐᒧᑦ ᐊᓇᐃᑦ
ptarmigan droppings

aqiggimut tumiit ᐊᖅᐱᕐᒧᑦ ᑐᒦᑦ
ptarmigan tracks

aqiggiq ᐊᖅᐱᕐᖅ *ptarmigan*

aqittuq ᐊᖅᐱᑦᑐᖅ *soft*

aqpik ᐊᖅᐱᒃ *cloudberry*

aqqusaarniaqtagit
ᐊᖅᒍᓵᕐᓂᐊᖅᑕᒋᑦ
I will pick you up along the way.

aqqusautiniaqtagit
ᐊᖅᒍᓴᐅᑎᓂᐊᖅᑕᒋᑦ
I will drop you off along the way.

aqqut ᐊᖅᒍᑦ *street*

aquttunnaqtuq ᐊᖅᐅᑦᑐᓐᓇᖅᑐᖕᒐ
He/she knows how to drive.

aqsarniit ᐊᖅᓴᕐᓃᑦ *northern lights*

aqua ᐊᖅᒐᐊ *the stern of a boat*

aquti ᐊᖅᒍᑎ *pilot*

arraagu ᐊᕐᒑᒍ *year / next year*

arraani ᐊᕐᒑᓂ *last year*

Arviat ᐊᕐᕕᐊᑦ *Arviat*

arvik ᐊᕐᕕᒃ *bowhead whale*

asukuluk ᐊᓱᑯᓗᒃ
That's very good to hear.

ataaniittuq ᐊᑖᓃᑦᑐᖅ
it's underneath

ataata ᐊᑖᑕ *father*

ataatatsiaq ᐊᑖᑦᓯᐊᖅ *grandfather*

atajuq ᐊᑕᔪᖅ *dress*

atausiq ᐊᑕᐅᓯᖅ *one*

atigi ᐊᑎᒋ
caribou parka with fur inside

atii ᐊᑏ *Let's go.*

atiliuqtara ᐊᑎᓕᐅᖅᑕᕋ
I signed it.

attunaaq ᐊᑦᑐᓈᖅ *rope*

aujaq ᐊᐅᔭᖅ *summer*

aujuittuq ᐊᐅᔪᐃᑦᑐᖅ *glacier*

auk ᐊᐅᒃ *blood*

aulautit ᐊᐅᓚᐅᑎᑦ
outboard motor

aullaqsimajuq ᐊᐅᓪᓚᖅᓯᒪᔪᖅ
He/she's out of town.

aunaaqtunga ᐊᐅᓈᖅᑐᖕᒐ
I am bleeding.

aupajaangajuq ᐊᐅᐸᔮᖓᔪᖅ
orange

aupaqtuq ᐊᐅᐸᖅᑐᖅ *red*

Ausuittuq ᐊᐅᓱᐃᑦᑐᖅ *Grise Fiord*

avalu ᐊᕙᓗ *wall*

avalumiutaq ᐊᕙᓗᒥᐅᑕᖅ
wall hanging

avatit ᐊᕙᑎᑦ *twenty*

avinngannguaq ᐊᕕᓐᖓᓐᖑᐊᖅ
mouse (computer)

avinngaq ᐊᕕᓐᖓᖅ *lemming*

guulu ᒎᓗ *gold*

haakiqtuq ᕼᐊᑭᖅᑐᖅ
He/she plays hockey.

haakirvik ᕼᐊᑭᕐᕕᒃ *hockey arena*

Haamalakkut ᕼᐊᒪᓚᒃᑯᑦ
hamlet office

hai? ᓴᐊᐃᐱ?   *What did you say?*

I

iga ᐊᒐ   *stove*

igalaangujaq ᐊᒐᓛᖑᔭᖅ
screen / monitor (computer)

igalaaq ᐊᒐᓛᖅ   *window*

iglua ᐊᖬᐊ
*the other one of a pair;
the matching one*

iglugiik ᐊᖬᒌᒃ   *pair*

igluinnaq ᐊᖬᐃᓐᓇᖅ   *one of a pair*

Igluligaarjuk ᐊᖬᓕᒑᕐᔪᒃ
Chesterfield Inlet

Iglulik ᐊᖬᓕᒃ   *Igloolik*

igunaq ᐊᔪᓇᖅ
fermented walrus meat

ii ᐄ   *yes*

iijagaq ᐄᔭᒐᖅ   *pill*

iijagaqtaarvik ᐄᔭᒐᖅᑖᕐᕕᒃ
pharmacy

iipuri ᐄᐳᕆ   *April*

iiqai ᐄᖃᐃ   *possibly*

iit ᐄᑦ   *eight*

iji ᐊᔨ   *eye*

ikiaqtiq ᐃᑭᐊᖅᑎᖅ   *shirt*

ikigit ᐃᑭᒋᑦ
Get in; Get on (command)

ikiguk ᐃᑭᒍᒃ   *Turn it on (command)*

ikiq ᐃᑭᖅ   *narrow passage / strait*

Ikpiarjuk ᐃᒃᐱᐊᕐᔪᒃ   *Arctic Bay*

ikulliaqtuq ᐃᑯᓪᓕᐊᖅᑐᖅ
There's no wind.

ikumajuq ᐃᑯᒪᔪᖅ   *It's turned on.*

ikumat ᐃᑯᒪᑦ   *matches*

ikusik ᐃᑯᓯᒃ   *elbow*

ilaali ᐃᓛᓕ   *you're welcome*

ilaannikkut ᐃᓛᓐᓂᒃᑯᑦ   *sometimes*

ilagiit ᐃᓚᒌᑦ   *family*

ilakka ᐃᓚᒃᑲ   *my family*

ilattinni ᐃᓚᑦᑎᓂ
At my relatives' place.

ilaujumavit? ᐃᓚᐅᔪᒪᕕᑦ?
Do you want to come along?

ilaujunnaqpunga?
ᐃᓚᐅᔪᓐᓇᖅᐳᖓ?
May I come along?

iliapan ᐃᓕᐊᐸᓐ   *eleven*

Ilinniaqtulirijikkut
ᐃᓕᓐᓂᐊᖅᑐᓕᕆᔨᒃᑯᑦ
Dept. of Education

ilinniarvik ᐃᓕᓐᓂᐊᕐᕕᒃ   *school*

iliragijara ᐃᓕᕋᒋᔭᕋ.
I'm afraid to disappoint him/her.

ilisaiji ᐃᓕᓴᐃᔨ   *teacher*

ilissinni ᐃᓕᔅᓯᓂ   *at your place*

ilitsi ᐃᓕᑦᓯ   *you (3 or more people)*

ilitsik ᐃᓕᑦᓯᒃ   *you (2 people)*

ilitsili? ᐃᓕᑦᓯᓕ?   *and you? (3 +)*

ilitsilli? ᐃᓕᑦᓯᓪᓕ?   *and you two?*

illu ᐃᓪᓗ   *house*

illuinaqtuut ᐃᓪᓗᐃᓇᖅᑑᑦ   *gun*

illuit allavviit ᐃᓪᓗᐃᑦ ᐊᓪᓚᕝᕖᑦ
office building

illuit atajut ᐃᓪᓗᐃᑦ ᐊᑕᔪᑦ
apartment building

illukutaat ᐃᓪᓗᑯᑖᑦ *row house*

illuralaaq ᐃᓪᓗᕋᓛᖅ *cabin*

illurusiq ᐃᓪᓗᕈᓯᖅ *bedroom*

iluani ᐃᓗᐊᓂ *inside*

iluaniittuq ᐃᓗᐊᓃᑦᑐᖅ *it's inside of*

iluiliq ᐃᓗᐃᓕᖅ *mainland*

imaq ᐃᒪᖅ *an expanse of water*

imaup sinaa ᐃᒪᐅᑉ ᓯᓈ *seashore*

imiq ᐃᒥᖅ *water (for drinking)*

imiqqutailaq ᐃᒥᖅᑯᑕᐃᓚᖅ
arctic tern

imiralavvik ᐃᒥᕋᓚᕝᕕᒃ *bar*

imirumajunga ᐃᒥᕈᒪᔪᖓ
I would like water.

immaqa ᐃᒻᒪᖃ *maybe*

immattuq ᐃᒻᒪᑦᑐᖅ *It is infected.*

immuk ᐃᒻᒧᒃ *milk*

immulisuungujunga ᐃᒻᒧᓕᓲᖑᔪᖓ
I take milk in my coffee/tea.

ingingaalirluk ᐃᖏᖠᓕᕐᓗᒃ
Let's sit down.

ingittiarit ᐃᖏᑦᑎᐊᕆᑦ
Please sit down.

ingiulittuq ᐃᖏᐅᓕᑦᑐᖅ
large swells (ocean)

inissaliuqtuq ᐃᓂᔅᓴᓕᐅᖅᑐᖅ
She/he makes an appointment.

inissaq ᐃᓂᔅᓴᖅ *appointment*

innaaruq ᐃᓐᓈᕈᖅ *cliff*

innaq ᐃᓐᓇᖅ *cigarette lighter*

innatiqtunga ᐃᓐᓇᑎᖅᑐᖓ
I go to bed.

inngiqti ᐃᙱᖅᑎ *singer*

inngirut ᐃᙱᕈᑦ *accordion*

inuktituusuungujunga
ᐃᓄᒃᑎᑑᓲᖑᔪᖓ
I speak Inuktitut.

inuktituusuunguviit?
ᐃᓄᒃᑎᑑᓲᖑᕖᑦ?
Do you speak Inuktitut?

inuttiavaaluk ᐃᓄᑦᑎᐊᕚᓗᒃ
He/she is a good person.

inuuqanniqtualuk
ᐃᓅᖃᓐᓂᖅᑐᐊᓗᒃ
She is easy to get along with.

iparaut ᐃᐸᕋᐅᑦ *dog whip*

ipiutat ᐃᐱᐅᑕᑦ *dog traces*

ippassaani ᐃᑉᐸᔅᓵᓂ
the day before yesterday

ippassaq ᐃᑉᐸᔅᓴᖅ *yesterday*

ippiarjuk ᐃᑉᐱᐊᕐᔪᒃ *pocket*

ipuut ᐃᐴᑦ *paddle; oar*

iqailisaqtuq ᐃᖃᐃᓕᓴᖅᑐᖅ
He/she exercises.

iqalliaqtunga ᐃᖃᓪᓕᐊᖅᑐᖓ
I am going fishing.

iqaluk ᐃᖃᓗᒃ *fish / char*

iqaluktaarvik ᐃᖃᓗᒃᑖᕐᕕᒃ
fish store

Iqaluktuuttiaq ᐃᖃᓗᒃᑑᑦᑎᐊᖅ
Cambridge Bay

Iqalummiutaujunga
ᐃᖃᓗᒻᒥᐅᑕᐅᔪᖓ.
I'm from Iqaluit; I live in Iqaluit

iqisulik ᐃᕿᓱᓕᒃ *curly hair*

iqqanaijakkaniqtunga
ᐃᖅᑲᓇᐃᔭᒃᑲᓂᖅᑐᖓ
I work some more.

iqqanaijaqtuq ᐃᖅᑲᓇᐃᔭᖅᑐᖅ
He/she works.

iqqanaijariaqtuq ᐃᖅᑲᓇᐃᔭᕆᐊᖅᑐᖅ
He/she goes to work.

iqqanaijariiqtuq ᐃᖅᑲᓇᐃᔭᕇᖅᑐᖅ
He/she finishes working.

iqqanaijariiruma ᐃᖅᑲᓇᐃᔭᕇᕈᒪ
when I am done work

iqqaqtuivik ᐃᖅᑲᖅᑐᐃᕕᒃ
courthouse

iqqaumaviit? ᐃᖅᑲᐅᒪᕖᑦ?
Do you remember?

iqsaq ᐃᖅᓴᖅ *cheek (by the nose)*

iquutit ᐃᕐᑰᑎᑦ *seaweed (frilly)*

irngiinaaqtaut ᐃᕐᖏᓈᖅᑕᐅᑦ *email*

irngusiq ᐃᕐᖑᓯᖅ *cup; mug*

irngutaq ᐃᕐᖑᑕᖅ *grandchild*

irniq ᐃᕐᓂᖅ *son*

isigak ᐃᓯᒐᒃ *foot*

isigaujaak ᐃᓯᒐᐅᔮᒃ *shoes*

isiqtunga ᐃᓯᖅᑐᖓ *I go in.*

isiriut ᐃᓯᕆᐅᑦ *button*

isumajunnailittiaqtunga ᐃᓱᒪᔪᓐᓇᐃᓕᑦᑎᐊᖅᑐᖓ
I can't think anymore.

isuraqtujuq ᐃᓱᕋᖅᑐᔪᖅ
lead dog (dog team)

itimak ᐃᑎᒪᒃ *palm of the hand*

ittaq ᐃᑦᑕᖅ *traditional skin tent*

ittinnguaq ᐃᑦᑎᙴᐊᖅ *purple*

ittirvik ᐃᑦᑎᕐᕕᒃ *luggage*

ittuq ᐃᑦᑐᖅ *grandfather*

ivalu ᐃᕙᓗ *sinew*

iviangiik ᐃᕕᐊᖀᒃ *breasts*

ivvilli? ᐃᕝᕕᓪᓕ?
and you? (1 person)

ivvillikiaq? ᐃᕝᕕᓪᓕᑭᐊᖅ?
What about you?

ivvit ᐃᕝᕕᑦ *you (1 person)*

J

jaa ᔮ *jam*

jaannuari ᔮᓐᓄᐊᕆ *January*

jaikak ᔭᐃᑲᒃ *jacket*

jaikaktariik ᔭᐃᑲᒃᑕᕇᒃ *suit*

jiulu ᔨᐅᓗ *zero*

julai ᔪᓚᐃ *July*

juuni ᔫᓂ *June*

K

kaaktunga ᑳᒃᑐᖓ *I am hungry.*

kaallariliqtunga ᑳᓪᓚᕆᓕᖅᑐᖓ
I'm famished.

kaapi ᑳᐱ *coffee*

kaapiliuqtunga ᑳᐱᓕᐅᖅᑐᖓ
I make coffee.

kaapitalik ᑳᐱᑕᓕᒃ.
There's coffee made.

kaapituqtunga ᑳᐱᑐᖅᑐᖓ
I drink coffee.

kaapiturumajunga ᑳᐱᑐᕈᒪᔪᖓ
I would like coffee.

kaapiturvik ᑳᐱᑐᕐᕕᒃ *coffee shop*

kajjaanaqtuq ᑲᔾᔮᓇᖅᑐᖅ
pleasant time or place

kajjiq ᑲᠵᠵᠢᠯᖅ *top of the head*

kajuq ᑲᠵᠢᒐ *brown*

kakiak ᑲᑭᐊᒃ *fork*

kallulik ᑲᓪᓗᓕᒃ *arctic loon*

kaluti ᑲᓗᑎ *hitch (qamutiik)*

kamaaluuk ᑲᒫᓘᒃ *rubber boots*

kamaaluuk ukiuqsiutiik
ᑲᒫᓘᒃ ᐅᑭᐅᖅᓯᐅᑏᒃ
winter boots

kamanaqtuq ᑲᒪᓇᖅᑐᖅ
It's amazing / unbelievable.

kamiik ᑲᒦᒃ *skin boots*

kamikutaak ᑲᒥᑯᑖᒃ *long boots*

kamillangillutit ᑲᒥᓪᓚᙳᓪᓗᑎᑦ
Please don't take your boots off.

kamillarlutit ᑲᒥᓪᓚᕐᓗᑎᑦ
Please take your boots off.

kanaak ᑲᓈᒃ *shin*

kanajuq ᑲᓇᔪᖅ *sculpin*

Kangiqłiniq ᑲᖏᖅᖠᓂᖅ
Rankin Inlet

Kangiqtugaapik ᑲᖏᖅᑐᒑᐱᒃ
Clyde River

kangiqtuk ᑲᖏᖅᑐᒃ *inlet; fiord*

kanguq ᑲᖑᖅ *snow goose*

kanngugijait ᑲᙲᒍᒋᔭᐃᑦ
He makes you feel shy.

kanngusuktutit ᑲᙲᓱᒃᑐᑎᑦ
You are feeling shy.

kappiagijanga ᑲᑉᐱᐊᒋᔭᖓ
He is scared of her.

kappiasuktunga ᑲᑉᐱᐊᓱᒃᑐᖓ
I am afraid.

katimajaqtuqsaalijunga
ᑲᑎᒪᔭᖅᑐᖅᓵᓕᔪᖓ
I'm early (for a meeting).

katimajaqturiaqarama
ᑲᑎᒪᔭᖅᑐᕆᐊᖃᕋᒪ
I have to go to a meeting.

katimajut ᑲᑎᒪᔪᑦ *They are meeting.*

katimavik ᑲᑎᒪᕕᒃ *boardroom*

Katturiarit! ᑲᑦᑐᕆᐊᕆᑦ! *Slow down!*

Kiap una? ᑭᐊᑉ ᐅᓇ?
Who does this belong to?

kiasik ᑭᐊᓯᒃ *shoulder blade*

kiati ᑭᐊᑎ *blouse*

kiattunga ᑭᐊᑦᑐᖓ *I am sweating.*

kigunniarvik ᑭᒍᓐᓂᐊᕐᕕᒃ
dentist's office

kigutangirnaq ᑭᒍᑕᖏᕐᓇᖅ
blueberry

kiguti ᑭᒍᑎ *tooth*

kiinaq ᑮᓇᖅ *face*

kiinaujakkuvik ᑮᓇᐅᔭᒃᑯᕕᒃ *bank*

kiinaujaq ᑮᓇᐅᔭᖅ *money*

kikiatsijjut ᑭᑭᐊᑦᓯᔾᔪᑦ *stapler*

kikkaq ᑭᒃᑲᖅ *bones with meat*

kikkajaktut ᑭᒃᑲᔭᒃᑐᑦ
they feast (on caribou bones).

kiliqtunga ᑭᓕᖅᑐᖓ *I cut myself.*

kiliugait ᑭᓕᐅᒑᐃᑦ *barnacles*

kimmik ᑭᒻᒥᒃ *heel*

kimminnaq ᑭᒻᒥᓐᓇᖅ *cranberry*

Kimmirut ᑭᒻᒥᕈᑦ *Kimmirut*

kina? ᑭᓇ? *Who?*

kinauva? ᑭᓇᐅᕙ? *What is his/her name?*

kingulliik ᑭᖑᓪᓕᒃ *hind leg*

kingulliqpaaq ᑭᖑᓪᓕᖅᐹᖅ *the last one*

kinguvaqqaujunga ᑭᖑᕙᖅᑲᐅᔪᖓ *I've arrived late (for a meeting).*

Kinngait ᑮᓐᖓᐃᑦ *Cape Dorset*

kinngait ᑮᓐᖓᐃᑦ *mountains*

kisaqsimajuq ᑭᓴᖅᓯᒪᔪᖅ *it is anchored*

kisarvik ᑭᓴᕐᕕᒃ *place to anchor*

kisaut ᑭᓴᐅᑦ *anchor*

kisiani ᑭᓯᐊᓂ *but*

kisulirijiugavilli? ᑭᓱᓕᕆᔨᐅᒐᕝᓕ? *And what do you do?*

Kisumit sanasimammat? ᑭᓱᒥᑦ ᓴᓇᓯᒪᒻᒪᑦ? *What's it made out of?*

kuanniq ᑯᐊᓐᓂᖅ *seaweed (long, fern-like)*

kujapigaq ᑯᔭᐱᒐᖅ *whale vertebrae*

kukkittapaarut ᑯᒃᑭᑦᑕᐹᕈᑦ *guitar*

kullu ᑯᓪᓗ *thumb*

Kuugaarjuk ᑰᒑᕐᔪᒃ *Kugaaruk*

kuugalaak ᑰᒐᓛᒃ *creek*

kuuk ᑰᒃ *river*

kuuqarvik ᑰᖃᕐᕕᒃ *kitchen*

M

ma'na ᒪᓇ *thank you (Kivalliq)*

maaniittuq ᒫᓃᑦᑐᖅ *It's around here.*

maanimiutaujunga ᒫᓂᒥᐅᑕᐅᔪᖓ. *I'm from here.*

maanna ᒫᓐᓇ *now*

maannaruluk ᒫᓐᓇᕈᓗᒃ *in a little while*

maatsi ᒫᑦᓯ *March*

mai ᒪᐃ *May*

maittuq ᒪᐃᑦᑐᖅ *It hurts.*

majuqqait ᒪᔪᖅᑲᐃᑦ *steep inclines*

majurautit ᒪᔪᕈᐊᑎᑦ *stairs; ladder*

makittaqtuq ᒪᑭᑦᑕᖅᑐᖅ *He/she plays cards.*

makittuq ᒪᑭᑦᑐᖅ *He/she gets out of bed.*

makuqtuq ᒪᑯᖅᑐᖅ *It's raining (N. Baffin)*

Maligalirijikkut ᒪᓕᒐᓕᕆᔨᒃᑯᑦ *Department of Justice*

malliqtuq ᒪᓪᓕᖅᑐᖅ *wavy*

mamarijara ᒪᒪᕆᔭᕋ *I like the taste of it.*

mamianaq ᒪᒥᐊᓇᖅ *sorry*

mannguumajuq ᒪᙳᒪᔪᖅ *mushy spring snow*

manniit ᒪᓐᓃᑦ *eggs*

marraq ᒪᕐᕋᖅ *mud on the ground*

marruliaminiuqatiqaqtunga ᒪᕈᓕᐊᒥᓂᐅᖃᑎᖃᖅᑐᖓ *I have a twin.*

marruuk ᒪᕐᕉᒃ *two*

mattaaq ᒪᑦᑖᖅ *skin of beluga or narwhal*

mattutissaqaqpit? ᒪᑦᑐᑎᔅᓴᖃᖅᐱᑦ? *Do you have a band-aid?*

matu ᒪᑐ *door*

128

matuingajuq ᒪᑐᐃᖓᔪᖅ
It is open.

matusimajuq ᒪᑐᓯᒪᔪᖅ
It is closed.

mauliqtuq ᒪᐅᓕᖅᑐᖅ
She / he hunts seals at their breathing holes.

mauna ᒪᐅᓇ *around here*

mikigaq ᒥᑭᒐᖅ *raw meat*

mikigaqtuqtut ᒥᑭᒐᖅᑐᖅᑐᑦ
they feast (on raw meat)

mikijumik ᒥᑭᔪᒥᒃ *a little bit*

mikijuq ᒥᑭᔪᖅ *small*

mikiluaqtuq ᒥᑭᓗᐊᖅᑐᖅ
It is too small.

minijuq ᒥᓂᔪᖅ *It's drizzling.*

miqsuqtuq ᒥᖅᓱᖅᑐᖅ *He/she sews.*

mirianngujunga ᒥᕆᐊᖖᒍᔪᖓ
I feel nauseous.

miriaqqaujunga ᒥᕆᐊᖅᑲᐅᔪᖓ
I threw up.

mirnguiqsirvik ᒥᕐᖑᐃᖅᓯᕐᕕᒃ *park*

mitiq ᒥᑎᖅ *duck*

mitsaanut ᒥᑦᓵᓄᑦ *about*

Mittimatalik ᒥᑦᑎᒪᑕᓕᒃ *Pond Inlet*

mumiqtuq ᒨᒥᖅᑐᖅ *He/she dances.*

mumiriaqtunga ᒨᒥᕆᐊᖅᑐᖓ
I go dancing.

mumirluk ᒨᒥᕐᓗᒃ *Let's dance.*

mumirumavit? ᒨᒥᕈᒪᕕᑦ?
Do you want to dance?

N

naalaut ᓈᓚᐅᑦ *radio*

naalautiqarvik ᓈᓚᐅᑎᖃᕐᕕᒃ
radio station

naalautittuq ᓈᓚᐅᑎᑦᑐᖅ
He/she listens to the radio.

naammattuq ᓈᒻᒪᑦᑐᖅ *it's O.K.*

naanngujuq ᓈᖖᒍᔪᖅ
has a stomach ache (he/she)

naaq ᓈᖅ *stomach*

naasauti ᓈᓴᐅᑎ *number*

naattiinguja ᓈᑦᑏᖑᔭ *Sunday*

naggajjau ᓇᒡᒐᑦᔭᐅ *Monday*

nagguarmik ᓇᒡᒍᐊᕐᒥᒃ *ring*

nain ᓇᐃᓐ *nine*

naittuq ᓇᐃᑦᑐᖅ *short*

najak ᓇᔭᒃ *sister of a male*

najjuk ᓇᕐᔪᒃ *antler*

nakurmiik ᓇᑯᕐᒦᒃ
thank you (S. Baffin)

nallaqtunga ᓇᓪᓚᖅᑐᖓ
I lie down.

nalligijara ᓇᓪᓕᒋᔭᕋ
I love her / him.

nalligivagit ᓇᓪᓕᒋᕙᒋᑦ *I love you.*

nalliuniqsiuqtuq ᓇᓪᓕᐅᓂᖅᓯᐅᖅᑐᖅ
having a birthday party

nami? ᓇᒥ? *where?*

namiippa? ᓇᒦᑉᐸ? *Where is it?*

namimiussajauvit?
ᓇᒥᒦᐅᔅᓴᔭᐅᕕᑦ?
Where are you originally from?

namimiutauva? ᓇᒥᒦᐅᑕᐅᕙ?
Where is she/he from; Where does she/he live?

nammagaaq ᓇᒻᒪᒑᖅ *knapsack*

namunngaqpit? ᓇᒧᙵᖅᐱᑦ? *Where are you going?*

nanniaqtuq ᓇᓐᓂᐊᖅᑐᖅ *She/he is hunting polar bear.*

nanuq ᓇᓄᖅ *polar bear*

nanuraq ᓇᓄᕋᖅ *polar bear fur*

nanurmut tumiit ᓇᓄᕐᒧᑦ ᑐᒦᑦ *bear tracks*

napu ᓇᐳ *wooden cross-bar (qamutiik)*

naqittaqtuq ᓇᕿᑦᑕᖅᑐᖅ *snaps (clothing)*

naqittaut ᓇᕿᑦᑕᐅᑦ *keyboard*

nasaruvaaq ᓇᓴᕈᕚᖅ *scarf (kercheif)*

naqsaq ᓇᖅᓴᖅ *valley*

nasaq ᓇᓴᖅ *hat*

natiruviaqtuq ᓇᑎᕈᕕᐊᖅᑐᖅ *drifting snow*

Natsilik ᓇᑦᓯᓕᒃ *coast between Kugaaruk & Gjoa Haven*

nattiq ᓇᑦᑎᖅ *ringed seal*

nattiqtuq ᓇᑦᑎᖅᑐᖅ *caught a ringed seal (he/she)*

nattirasugiaqtuq ᓇᑦᑎᕋᓱᒋᐊᖅᑐᖅ *She / he is hunting seal.*

nattivak ᓇᑦᑎᕙᒃ *hooded seal*

Naujaat ᓇᐅᔮᑦ *Repulse Bay*

naujaq ᓇᐅᔭᖅ *seagull*

naukkut? ᓇᐅᒃᑯᑦ? *Where?*

niaqunngujuq ᓂᐊᖁᙳᔪᖅ *has a headache (he/she)*

Niaqunnguut ᓂᐊᖁᙴᑦ *Apex*

niaquq ᓂᐊᖁᖅ *head*

nijjaajut ᓂᔾᔮᔪᑦ *music*

nijjausijaqtit ᓂᔾᔭᐅᓯᔭᖅᑎᑦ *musicians; band*

nijjausijaqtuq ᓂᔾᔭᐅᓯᔭᖅᑐᖅ *He/she plays music.*

nikkuk ᓂᒃᑯᒃ *dried meat*

nillasuktuq ᓂᓪᓚᓱᒃᑐᖅ *cold weather*

nillirajuittuq ᓂᓪᓕᕋᔪᐃᑦᑐᖅ *He/she is very quiet.*

ningiuq ᓂᖏᐅᖅ *grandmother*

ninngassaraittuq ᓂᙵᔅᓴᕋᐃᑦᑐᖅ *He/she has a quick temper.*

ninngaumajunga ᓂᙵᐅᒪᔪᖓ *I am angry.*

niqtiuqtunga ᓂᖅᑎᐅᖅᑐᖓ *I am cooking.*

nirigiiqqaujunga ᓂᕆᒌᖅᑲᐅᔪᖓ *I've already eaten.*

nirijuq ᓂᕆᔪᖅ *He/she eats.*

nirivijjuaq ᓂᕆᕕᔾᔪᐊᖅ *community feast*

nirivik ᓂᕆᕕᒃ *restaurant; dining room*

nirlik ᓂᕐᓕᒃ *Canada goose*

nittaittuq ᓂᑦᑕᐃᑦᑐᖅ *weather with low visibility*

niu ᓂᐅ *leg*

niuviqtuq ᓂᐅᕕᖅᑐᖅ *He/she buys.*

niuviriaqtunga ᓂᐅᕕᕆᐊᖅᑐᖓ *I go shopping.*

niuvirvik ᓂᐅᕕᕐᕕᒃ *store*

niuvirviralaaq ᓂᐅᕕᕐᕕᕋᓛᖅ *corner store*

nuijagaq ᓄᐃᔭᒐᖅ *sweater*

nujakittuq ᓄᔭᑭᑦᑐᖅ *short hair*

nujakutaak ᓄᔭᑯᑖᒃ *long hair*

nujangit qirniqtut ᓄᔭᖕᒉ ᖅᐱᕐᓂᖅᑐᑦ
dark hair

nujangit qurjut ᓄᔭᖕᒉ ᖁᕐᔪᑦ
light hair

nujat ᓄᔭᑦ *hair*

nukaq ᓄᑲᖅ
younger sibling (of same sex)

nukillausiriji ᓄᑭᓪᓚᐅᓯᕆᔨ
electrician

nuliaq ᓄᓕᐊᖅ *wife*

nulu ᓄᓗ *buttock*

numaagijanga ᓄᒫᒋᔭᖕᒐ
It makes him sad.

nuna ᓄᓇ *land*

nunalik ᓄᓇᓕᒃ *community*

nunarait ᓄᓇᕌᐃᑦ *flowers*

nunasiuqtuq ᓄᓇᓯᐅᖅᑐᖅ
He/she drives a car.

Nunatsiaq ᓄᓇᑦᓯᐊᖅ
Northwest Territories

Nunatsiavut ᓄᓇᑦᓯᐊᕗᑦ *Labrador*

Nunavik ᓄᓇᕕᒃ *Nunavik*

nuqarutit ᓄᖃᕈᑏᑦ
ropes for securing a tent

nuqqangajuq ᓄᖅᖃᖕᒐᔪᖅ
still; motionless

Nuqqarit! ᓄᖅᖃᕆᑦ! *Stop!*

nuvattuq ᓄᕙᑦᑐᖅ
He/she has a cold.

nuvipiri ᓄᕕᐱᕆ *November*

nuvua ᓄᕗᐊ *point*

nuvuja ᓄᕗᔭ *cloud*

nuvujajuq ᓄᕗᔭᔪᖅ *It's cloudy.*

P

paa ᐹ *entrance way; door*

paallaktuq ᐹᓪᓚᒃᑐᖅ
He/she stumbles.

paatiriaqtunga ᐹᑎᕆᐊᖅᑐᖓ
I'm going to a party.

pai ᐸᐃ *five*

paiggaala ᐸᐃᒡᒑᓚ *gas can*

paippaamuurijjut ᐸᐃᑉᐹᒨᕆᔾᔪᑦ
printer

paippaaq ᐸᐃᑉᐹᖅ *paper*

pairivik ᐸᐃᕆᕕᒃ *daycare*

palaugaaq ᐸᓚᐅᒑᖅ *bannock*

palaugaaqtuqtunga
ᐸᓚᐅᒑᖅᑐᖅᑐᖓ
I am eating bannock.

paliaq ᐸᓕᐊᖅ *plate*

paliisi ᐸᓖᓯ *police*

paliisikkut ᐸᓖᓯᒃᑯᑦ
police department

panik ᐸᓂᒃ *daughter*

paniqtuq ᐸᓂᖅᑐᖅ *dry*

Panniqtuuq ᐸᓐᓂᖅᑑᖅ *Pangnirtung*

parnattuq ᐸᕐᓇᑦᑐᖅ
He/she prepares to depart.

patiujaq ᐸᑎᐅᔭᖅ *candle*

patuttuq ᐸᑐᑦᑐᖅ *There's ice fog.*

patuutalik ᐸᑑᑕᓕᒃ
light dusting of snow

paurngaq ᐸᐅᕐᖓᖅ *crowberry*

pautiik ᐸᐅᑏᒃ *kayak paddle*

pavvik ᐸᵛᕕᒃ *wrist*

piamik ∧ᐊᒥᑉ *a beer*

piana ∧ᐊᑲ *piano*

piga ∧ᑯ *It's mine.*

piit? ᐱᑉ? *Is it your's?*

pijariillariliraluaqtunga
∧ᔮᓐᓪᓚᓕᕐᓱᐊᖅᑐᖕᓗ
I am almost done.

pijariiqsimajuq ∧ᔮᓐᖅᓯᒪᔪᖅ
It is ready; it is finished.

pijariiqtunga ∧ᔮᓐᖅᑐᖕᓗ *I'm done.*

pijassaqaluaqpit? ∧ᔭᓴᖅᓗᐊᖅᐱᑦ?
Are you too busy?

pijassaqaluaqtunga
∧ᔭᓴᖅᓗᐊᖅᑐᖕᓗ
I am very busy.

pijikataaq ∧ᔭᑲᑖᖅ *waiter*

pijikataat ∧ᔭᑲᑖᑦ *in-flight crew*

pilirijara ∧ᓕᑎᔭᕋ
I am working on it.

pinasuarusilimaaq ∧ᓇᓱᐊᐳᓯᓕᒫᖅ
all week

pinasuarusiq ∧ᓇᓱᐊᐳᓯᖅ *week*

pinasuarusiulaaqtuq
∧ᓇᓱᐊᐳᓯᐅᓛᖅᑐᖅ
next week

pinasuarusiulauqtuq
∧ᓇᓱᐊᐳᓯᐅᓚᐅᖅᑐᖅ
last week

pinasuarusiup nunnguani
∧ᓇᓱᐊᐳᓯᐅᑉ ᓄᖕᖑᐊᓂ
on the weekend

pingasut ∧ᖓᓱᑦ *three*

pingasuujuqtut ∧ᖓᓱᔪᖅᑐᑦ *six*

pingatsiq ∧ᖓᑦᓯᖅ *Wednesday*

pinikisautijut ∧ᓂᑭᓴᐅᑎᔪᑦ
competitions

pinnguaq ∧ᖕᖑᐊᖅ *game*

pinnguaqtuq ∧ᖕᖑᐊᖅᑐᖅ
He/she plays a game.

pinnguarvik ∧ᖕᖑᐊᕐᕕᒃ
recreational centre

piqataujumaviit? ∧ᖅᑕᐅᔪᒪᕖᑦ?
Do you want to come along?

piqsiqtuq ∧ᖅᓯᖅᑐᖅ *It's blizzarding.*

pirraak ∧ᕐᕌᒃ *qamutiik runners*

pirunaqsaqtuq ∧ᕈᓇᖅᓴᖅᑐᖅ
He/she cleans up.

piruqtut ∧ᕈᖅᑐᑦ *plants*

pirut ∧ᕈᑦ *rocks for securing a tent*

pisuktit ∧ᓱᒃᑎᑦ *land animals*

pisuktuq ∧ᓱᒃᑐᖅ *He/she walks.*

pisuutikkut tisamalikkut
∧ᓲᑎᒃᑯᑦ ᑎᓴᒪᓕᒃᑯᑦ
by four-wheeler

pitti ∧ᑎ *dried fish*

pittiulaaq ∧ᑎᐅᓚᖅ
black guillemot

piturnivik ∧ᑐᕐᓂᕕᒃ
tide at full moon

piugijara ∧ᐅᒋᔭᕋ *I like it.*

piujuq ∧ᐅᔪᖅ *good*

piuniqsaq ∧ᐅᓂᖅᓴᖅ *better*

pua ᐳᐊ *four*

pualuuk ᐳᐊᓘᒃ *(pair of) mittens*

puigurassaungittuq
ᐳᐃᒍᕋᓱᖅᐴᖕᑦᑐᖅ
It's hard to forget.

puiji ᐳᐃᔨ
*any sea mammal that pops its
head out of the water*

pukajaak ᐳᑲᔮᒃ
  old snow (hard like ice)

pulaaqtiqaqtunga ᐳᓛᖅᑎᖃᖅᑐᖓ
  I have a visitor.

pulaarvik ᐳᓛᕐᕕᒃ   *living room*

punnirniq ᐳᓐᓂᕐᓂᖅ
  boiled caribou fat (hardened)

puqtujut ᐳᖅᑐᔪᑦ   *highlands*

putuguq ᐳᑐᒍᖅ   *toe*

puuq ᐳᖅ   *bag; sack; sleeping bag*

Q

qaanganiittuq ᖃᖓᓅᑦᑐᖅ
  it's on top of

qagaaqtuq ᖃᒑᖅᑐᖅ   *whitecaps*

qaijjaanngittunga ᖃᐃᔾᔮᙱᑦᑐᖓ
  I won't be coming

qainiaqtunga ᖃᐃᓂᐊᖅᑐᖓ
  I'll be there.

qaiqsugaaq ᖃᐃᖅᓱᒑᖅ
  rocky ground

qairulik ᖃᐃᕈᓕᒃ   *harp seal*

qajaq ᖃᔭᖅ   *kayak*

qajuq ᖃᔪᖅ   *broth*

qaksungaut ᖃᒃᓱᖓᐅᑦ
  tie for the amauti

qakuguttauq ᖃᑯᒍᑦᑕᐅᖅ
  until next time

qakuqtuq ᖃᑯᖅᑐᖅ   *white*

qalasiq ᖃᓚᓯᖅ   *belly button*

qalipaaq ᖃᓕᐸᖅ   *sweater*

qaliralik ᖃᓕᕋᓕᒃ   *turbot*

qallu ᖃᙶ   *eyebrow*

qallunaujasuunguvit? ᖃᓪᓗᓇᐅᔭᓲᖑᕕᑦ?
  Do you speak English?

Qamani'tuaq ᖃᒪᓂᑦᑐᐊᖅ
  Baker Lake

qamiguk ᖃᒥᒍᒃ
  Turn it off (command)

qaminngajuq ᖃᒥᙶᔪᖅ
  It's turned off.

qamutaujakkut ᖃᒧᑕᐅᔭᒃᑯᑦ
  by snowmobile

qamutaujaq ᖃᒧᑕᐅᔭᖅ
  snowmobile

qamutaujaqtuq ᖃᒧᑕᐅᔭᖅᑐᖅ
  He/she drives a snowmobile.

qamutiik ᖃᒧᑏᒃ   *kamotik; sled*

qanga? ᖃᖓ?   *when?*

Qangakkut nalliutisuunguvit? ᖃᖓᒃᑯᑦ ᓇᓪᓕᐅᑎᓲᖑᕕᑦ?
  When is your birthday?

qangatasuukkuvik ᖃᖓᑕᓲᒃᑯᕕᒃ
  airport

qangatasuuq ᖃᖓᑕᓲᖅ   *airplane*

qangatasuuqti ᖃᖓᑕᓲᖅᑎ   *pilot*

qangattaut ᖃᖓᑦᑕᐅᑦ
  airline ticket

qangattiaq ᖃᖓᑦᑎᐊᖅ   *soon*

qanimajunga ᖃᓂᒪᔪᖓ
  I am sick.

qaniq ᖃᓂᖅ   *mouth*

qanittuq ᖃᓂᑦᑐᖅ   *near; close*

qanitturuluk ᖃᓂᑦᑐᕈᓗᒃ
  It's close.

qanniqtuq ᖃᓐᓂᖅᑐᖅ
  It's snowing.

qanuigiviuk? ᖃᓄᐃᒋᕕᐅᒃ?
  How do you feel about him/her?

qanuinngittuq ᖃᓄᐃᙱᑦᑐᖅ
She/he is fine.

qanuippit? ᖃᓄᐃᐱᑦ?
How are you?

qanuq? ᖃᓄᖅ?
how?

Qanurli isumagiviuk?
ᖃᓄᕐᓕ ᐃᓱᒪᒋᕕᐅᒃ?
What do you think of him/her?

Qanurli isumavit? ᖃᓄᕐᓕ ᐃᓱᒪᕕᑦ
What do you think?

qanuruuq? ᖃᓄᕈᖅ?
What did you say?

qanutigi? ᖃᓄᑎᒋ? for how long?

qapilagijara ᖃᐱᓚᒋᔭᕋ
I find it dreary.

qaqqajaaq ᖃᖅᖃᔮᖅ hill

qaqqaq ᖃᖅᖃᖅ mountain

qaqtu ᖃᖅᑐ lower lip

qarasaujaq ᖃᕋᓴᐅᔭᖅ computer

qarasaujaralaaq ᖃᕋᓴᐅᔭᕋᓛᖅ
laptop

qarlialuuk ᖃᕐᓕᐊᓘᒃ wind pants

qarliik ᖃᕐᓖᒃ pants

qarlikallaak ᖃᕐᓕᑲᓪᓛᒃ skin pants

qasigiaq ᖃᓯᒋᐊᖅ harbour seal

qatannguti ᖃᑕᙳᑎ sibling

Qatsinik qatanngutiqaqpit?
ᖃᑦᓯᓂᒃ ᖃᑕᙳᑎᖃᖅᐱᑦ?
How many siblings do you have?

qatsungaut ᖃᑦᓱᖕᐅᑦ
tie for an amauti

qattimuuqpa? ᖃᑦᑎᒨᖅᐸ?
What time is it?

qattimuuqpat? ᖃᑦᑎᒨᖅᐸᑦ?
at what time?

qattiriji ᖃᑦᑎᕆᔨ firefighter

qattirijikkut ᖃᑦᑎᕆᔨᒃᑯᑦ fire hall

qaujimagiarit! ᖃᐅᔨᒪᒋᐊᕆᑦ !
Watch out!

qaumat ᖃᐅᒪᑦ lights

qaummaqqut ᖃᐅᒻᒪᖅᑯᑦ
lamp

qauppalli? ᖃᐅᑉᐸᓪᓕ?
What about tomorrow?

qauppat ᖃᐅᑉᐸᑦ tomorrow

qauq ᖃᐅᖅ forehead

qausiqtuq ᖃᐅᓯᖅᑐᖅ wet

Qausuittuq ᖃᐅᓱᐃᑦᑐᖅ
Resolute Bay

qautamaat ᖃᐅᑕᒫᑦ every day

qavvik ᖃᕝᕕᒃ wolverine

qavvirajak ᖃᕝᕕᕋᔭᒃ wolverine fur

qiajuq ᕿᐊᔪᖅ He/she cries.

qiggiqtaqtuq ᕿᒡᒋᖅᑕᖅᑐᖅ
He/she is jumping.

qiiq ᕿᖅ white hair

Qikiqtaaluk ᕿᑭᖅᑖᓗᒃ
Baffin Island

qikiqtaq ᕿᑭᖅᑕᖅ island

Qikiqtarjuaq ᕿᑭᖅᑕᕐᔪᐊᖅ
Qikiqtarjuaq

qilak ᕿᓚᒃ sky

qilalugaq ᕿᓚᓗᒐᖅ
beluga (also narwhal in some
dialects)

qilalugaqtuq ᕿᓚᓗᒐᖅᑐᖅ
He/she caught a whale.

qilalukkiaqtuq ᕿᓚᓗᒃᑭᐊᖅᑐᖅ
He/she hunts whale.

qilliqtuq ᕿᒃᑕᖅ
CD (compact disk)

qiluaq ᕿᓗᐊᖅ *belt*

qimiriat ᕿᒥᕆᐊᑦ *eyelashes*

qimirluk ᕿᒥᕐᓗᒃ *spine*

qimmiq ᕿᒻᒥᖅ *dog*

qimussit ᕿᒧᔅᓯᑦ *dog team*

qingaq ᕿᖓᖅ *nose*

Qingaut ᕿᖓᐅᑦ *Bathurst Inlet*

qinnguq ᕿᙴᖅ *brow*

qinngut ᕿᙴᑦ *scope of a rifle*

qiqinnikuujunga ᕿᕿᓐᓂᑰᔪᖓ
I have frostbite.

qiqippallaijuminiujunga.
ᕿᕿᑉᐸᓪᓚᐃᔪᒥᓂᐅᔪᖓ.
I think I have frostbite.

qiqsuqqangajuq ᕿᖅᓱᖅᖃᖓᔪᖅ
*spring snow that softens during
the day & freezes at night*

qirniqtuq ᕿᕐᓂᖅᑐᖅ *black*

qisik ᕿᓯᒃ *skin (sea mamals)*

qitiq ᕿᑎᖅ *waist*

qitirluttunga ᕿᑎᕐᓗᑦᑐᖓ
I have a sore back.

Qitirmiut ᕿᑎᕐᒥᐅᑦ
Kitikmeot Region

qiturngaq ᕿᑐᕐᖓᖅ
one's own child

qiturngaqaqpit? ᕿᑐᕐᖓᖃᖅᐱᑦ?
Do you have any children?

qiujunga ᕿᐅᔪᖓ *I am cold.*

quakkuvik ᖁᐊᒃᑯᕕᒃ *freezer*

quana ᖁᐊᓇ
thank you (Inuinnaqtun)

quaq ᖁᐊᖅ *frozen meat*

quaqaut ᖁᐊᖃᐅᑦ *fridge*

quiqsuqtunga ᖁᐃᖅᓱᖅᑐᖓ
I am coughing.

qujannamiik ᖁᔭᓐᓇᒦᒃ
thank you (N. Baffin)

qujjaunnat ᖁᔾᔭᐅᓐᓇᑦ *eel*

qukiut ᖁᑭᐅᑦ *rifle*

qulaa kingulliq ᖁᓛ ᑭᖑᓪᓕᖅ
second floor

qulaa sivulliq ᖁᓛ ᓯᕗᓪᓕᖅ
first floor

qulaani ᖁᓛᓂ *noon*

qulaaniippa? ᖁᓛᓃᑉᐸ?
Is she/he/it upstairs?

qulaaniittuq ᖁᓛᓃᑦᑐᖅ
it's above

qulit ᖁᓕᑦ *ten*

qulittaq ᖁᓕᑦᑕᖅ
caribou parka with fur outside

qulittaujaq ᖁᓕᑦᑕᐅᔭᖅ
parka (contemporary)

quliunngigaqtut ᖁᓕᐅᙲᒐᖅᑐᑦ
nine

qungasiq ᖁᖓᓯᖅ *neck*

qungasiruq ᖁᖓᓯᕈᖅ
scarf; men's tie

qunguliit ᖁᖑᓖᑦ *mountain sorrel*

qupanuaq ᖁᐸᓄᐊᖅ *snow bunting*

quqsuqtuq ᖁᖅᓱᖅᑐᖅ *yellow*

Qurluqtuq ᖁᕐᓗᖅᑐᖅ *Kugluktuk*

qurlurniq ᖁᕐᓗᕐᓂᖅ *waterfall*

qusujunga ᖁᓱᔪᖓ *I am sad.*

qutturaq ᖁᑦᑐᕋᖅ *thigh*

quviagijara ᖁᕕᐊᒋᔭᕋ
I enjoy it.

quvianallarittuq ᖁᕕᐊᓇᓪᓚᕆᑦᑐᖅ
It's wonderful.

quviananngillarittuq
ᖁᕕᐊᓇᙱᓪᓚᕆᑦᑐᖅ
It's terrible.

quviasuktuq ᖁᕕᐊᓱᒃᑐᖅ
He/she happy.

quviasuppiit? ᖁᕕᐊᓱᑉᐲᑦ?
Are you happy?

quviasuusiaq ᖁᕕᐊᓲᓯᐊᖅ
Christmas present

S

saa ᓵ *table*

saanganiittuq ᓵᖓᓃᑦᑐᖅ
it's in front of

saattuujaut ᓵᑦᑑᔭᐅᑦ *frying pan*

saavittuq ᓵᕕᑦᑐᖅ *launching a boat*

saipan ᓴᐃᐸᓐ *seven*

sakkut ᓴᒃᑯᑦ *bullets*

Salliit ᓴᓪᓖᑦ *Coral Harbour*

sanannguagaq ᓴᓇᙳᐊᒐᖅ
carving

sanianiittuq ᓴᓂᐊᓃᑦᑐᖅ
it's beside

Sanikiluaq ᓴᓂᑭᓗᐊᖅ *Sanikiluaq*

Sanirajak ᓴᓂᕋᔭᒃ *Hall Beach*

saniraq ᓴᓂᕋᖅ *side (of body)*

sassi ᓴᔅᓯ *six*

saumik ᓴᐅᒥᒃ *left*

savik ᓴᕕᒃ *knife*

savvik ᓴᕝᕕᒃ *chest*

siarnaq ᓯᐊᕐᓇᖅ *grey*

siarrijautiik ᓯᐊᕐᕆᔭᐅᑏᒃ
snowmobile skis

siggaliaqtusuunguvit?
ᓯᒡᒐᓕᐊᖅᑐᓲᖑᕕᑦ?
Do you smoke?

siggaliat ᓯᒡᒐᓕᐊᑦ *cigarettes*

Siipiisiikkut ᓰᐲᓰᒃᑯᑦ
Canadian Broadcasting Corp (CBC)

siiqquq ᓰᖅᑯᖅ *knee*

sijja ᓯᔾᔭ *water's edge (land/ice)*

siksik ᓯᒃᓯᒃ *arctic ground squirrel*

siku ᓯᑯ *ice*

sikurlak ᓯᑯᕐᓚᒃ
snow where only the surface is iced up & hard

sila ᓯᓚ
weather; environment; the outdoors

silaluttuq ᓯᓚᓗᑦᑐᖅ
It's raining (S. Baffin)

silami ᓯᓚᒥ *outside*

silapaaq ᓯᓚᐹᖅ
outer shell of a parka

silaqqiqtuq ᓯᓚᖅᑭᖅᑐᖅ *clear skies*

silataaniittuq ᓯᓚᑖᓃᑦᑐᖅ
it's outside of

silattiavak ᓯᓚᑦᑎᐊᕙᒃ
good weather

sinaaniittuq ᓯᓈᓃᑦᑐᖅ
it's at the edge of

singirniq ᓯᖏᕐᓂᖅ *ankle*

siniliqtunga ᓯᓂᓕᖅᑐᖓ
I fall asleep.

sinittiaqqauvit? ᓯᓂᑦᑎᐊᖅᑲᐅᕕᑦ?
Did you sleep well?

sinivvik ᓯᓂᕝᕕᒃ *sleeping bag*

sinnatuqtuq ᓯᓐᓇᑐᖅᑐᖅ
He/she dreams.

siqiiq ᓯᕿᖅ *zipper*

siqiniq ᓯᕿᓂᖅ *sun*

siqiniq nipijuq ᓯᕿᓂᖅ ᓂᐱᔪᖅ
sunset

siqiniq nuijuq ᓯᕿᓂᖅ ᓄᐃᔪᖅ
sunrise

siqinniqtuq ᓯᕿᓐᓂᖅᑐᖅ
It is sunny.

siqquq ᓯᖅᑯᖅ *aged seal flipper*

sirluaq ᓯᕐᓗᐊᖅ *storage shed*

sitamat ᓯᑕᒪᑦ *four*

sitamaujunngigaqtut
ᓯᑕᒪᐅᔪᙱᒐᖅᑐᑦ *seven*

sitamaujuqtut ᓯᑕᒪᐅᔪᖅᑐᑦ *eight*

sitammiq ᓯᑕᒻᒥᖅ *Thursday*

sitipiri ᓯᑎᐱᕆ *September*

siummiutaak ᓯᐅᒻᒥᐅᑖᒃ *earrings*

siuraq ᓯᐅᕋᖅ *sand*

siut ᓯᐅᑦ *ear*

sivataarvik ᓯᕙᑖᕐᕕᒃ *Saturday*

sivaujaq ᓯᕙᐅᔭᖅ *cookie*

sivua ᓯᕗᐊ *bow of a boat*

sivulliqpaaq ᓯᕗᓪᓕᖅᐹᖅ
the first one

sivuraaniittuq ᓯᕗᕌᓃᑦᑐᖅ
it's in front of

sukalisuungujunga ᓱᑲᓕᓲᖑᔪᖓ.
I take sugar with my coffee/tea.

sukaq ᓱᑲᖅ *sugar*

Sukkaigialaurit! ᓱᒃᑲᐃᒋᐊᓚᐅᕆᑦ!
Slow down!

Sukkaillutit uqaruk.
ᓱᒃᑲᐃᓪᓗᑎᑦ ᐅᖃᕈᒃ.
Say it slowly.

sukkaittuq ᓱᒃᑲᐃᑦᑐᖅ *slow*

sukkajukkuurut ᓱᒃᑲᔪᒃᑰᕈᑦ
fax machine

sukkajuq ᓱᒃᑲᔪᖅ *fast*

sukuttianiippa? ᓱᑯᑦᑎᐊᓃᑉᐸ?
Where exactly is it?

sulaaqpit? ᓱᓛᖅᐱᑦ?
What will you be doing (tomorrow or later)?

suli ᓱᓕ *still (unchanged)*

summat? ᓱᒻᒪᑦ? *why?*

suniaqpit? ᓱᓂᐊᖅᐱᑦ?
What will you be doing later?

sunnaittuq ᓱᓐᓇᐃᑦᑐᖅ
stormy weather

supuujuq ᓱᐴᔪᖅ *camp stove*

surattuq ᓱᕋᑦᑐᖅ *It's broken.*

suva? ᓱᕙ? *What?*

suvaguuq? ᓱᕙᒎᖅ?
What did he/she say?

suvit? ᓱᕕᑦ?
What are you doing?

T

taatsi ᑖᑦᓯ *taxi*

taatsiiliqigiaqaqtunga
ᑖᑦᓰᓕᕿᒋᐊᖃᖅᑐᖓ
I need to call a taxi.

taatsiiliqijunga ᑖᑦᓰᓕᕿᔪᖓ
I am calling a cab.

Taika! ᑕᐃᑲ! *There it is!*

taikaniittuq ᑕᐃᑲᓂᐅᒡᑐᖅ
It is over there (specific spot)

tajan ᑕᔭ *ten*

takijuq ᑕᑭᔪᖅ *tall*

takujagaqarvik ᑕᑯᔭᖃᖅᕕᒃ
museum

takulaarivuguk ᑕᑯᓛᕆᕗᒍᒃ
We'll see you again. (to 1 person).

takuminaqsautit ᑕᑯᒥᓇᖅᓴᐅᑎᑦ
jewelry

talaviisaqtunga ᑕᓚᕖᓴᖅᑐᖕᒐ
I am watching TV.

taliannguaq ᑕᓕᐊᙳᐊᖅ *bracelet*

taliaq ᑕᓕᐊᖅ *wrist watch; bracelet*

talii ᑕᓕ *three*

taliq ᑕᓕᖅ *arm*

taliqpik ᑕᓕᖅᐱᒃ *right*

tallimat ᑕᓪᓕᒫᑦ *five*

tallirmiq ᑕᓪᓕᕐᒥᖅ *Friday*

tallurunnaq ᑕᓪᓗᕐᓈᖅ *scallop*

Talurjuaq ᑕᓗᕐᔪᐊᖅ *Taloyoak*

tamauna ᑕᒪᐅᓇ *Right here.*

tammariikkut ᑕᒻᒪᕖᒃᑯᑦ *GPS*

taqqiq ᑕᖅᑭᖅ *month*

taqqiulaaqtuq ᑕᖅᑭᐅᓛᖅᑐᖅ
next month

taqqiulauqtuq ᑕᖅᑭᐅᓚᐅᖅᑐᖅ
last month

tariuq ᑕᕆᐅᖅ *sea; salt*

tarrijarniaqtunga ᑕᕐᕆᔭᕐᓂᐊᖅᑐᖕᒐ
I'm going to watch a movie.

tarrijarvik ᑕᕐᕆᔭᕐᕕᒃ
movie theatre

tasiarjuk ᑕᓯᐊᕐᔪᒃ *pond*

tasiq ᑕᓯᖅ *lake*

tasiujaq ᑕᓯᐅᔭᖅ *bay*

tatsiqtuq ᑕᑦᓯᖅᑐᖅ *It is foggy.*

taunaniittuq ᑕᐅᓇᓂᐅᒡᑐᖅ
It is down there.

tauvaniittuq ᑕᐅᕙᓂᐅᒡᑐᖅ
It's over there (general area)

tavvauvusi ᑕᕝᕚᐅᕝᓯ
Good-bye (speaking to 3+)

tiguanguviit? ᑎᒍᐊᖑᕖᑦ?
Were you adopted?

tii ᑏ *tea*

tiiliuqtunga ᑏᓕᐅᖅᑐᖕᒐ
I am making tea.

tiituqtunga ᑏᑐᖅᑐᖕᒐ
I am drinking tea.

tiiturumajunga ᑏᑐᕈᒪᔪᖕᒐ.
I would like tea.

tikaagullik ᑎᑳᒍᓪᓕᒃ *minke whale*

tikiq ᑎᑭᖅ *index finger*

Tikirarjuaq ᑎᑭᕋᕐᔪᐊᖅ *Whale Cove*

timi ᑎᒥ *body*

timmiat ᑎᒻᒥᐊᑦ *birds*

tininngajuq ᑎᓂᙵᔪᖅ
It's low tide.

tiqqialik ᑎᖅᑭᐊᓕᒃ *baseball cap*

tiriaq ᑎᕆᐊᖅ *weasel*

tiriganiaq ᑎᕆᒐᓂᐊᖅ *arctic fox*

tiriganiarajak ᑎᕆᒐᓂᐊᕋᔭᒃ
fox fur

tisamat ᑎᓴᒫᑦ *four*

tisijuq ∩ᒃᓱᑉ *hard*

tisilluqaq ∩ᒃᓗᑉᒃᓱᑉ
hard packed snow

tisipiri ∩ᒃᓯᐱ *December*

titiqqaniarvik ∩∩ᔅᑉᑲᓂᐊᑦᕐᔾ
post office

titiqqaniarvimmuuqtunga
∩∩ᔅᑉᑲᓂᐊᑦᕐᔾᒨᖅᑐᖕᒐ
I go to the post office.

titiqqaq ∩∩ᔅᑉᑉ
letter; document; text

titiqtugaq ∩∩ᔅᑉᑐᒡᔅᑉ *print (artwork)*

titiraut ∩∩ᔅᐅᑦ *pen; pencil*

tuaju ᑐᐊᔾ *twelve*

tuapak ᑐᐊᑉ *gravel*

Tuavilaurit! ᑐᐊᕕᓚᐅᐱᑦ!
Hurry up!

tuaviriaqaliqtunga
ᑐᐊᕕᐱᐊᑲᓕᖅᑐᖕᒐ
I have to hurry.

tui ᑐᐃ *shoulder*

tujurmivik ᑐᔾᕐᒥᕝ *hotel*

tukimuatitsiji ᑐᑭᒨᐊᑎᑦᕐᔾ
director (job title)

tukisijuq ᑐᑭᓯᔪᑉ
He/she understands.

tulattuq ᑐᓚᑦᑐᑉ *landing a boat*

tulimaat ᑐᓕᒫᑦ *ribs*

tumiit ᑐᒦᑦ *tracks*

tungujuqtuq ᑐᖕᒍᔪᖅᑐᑉ *blue*

tunngasugit ᑐᖖᒐᓱᒋᑦ
welcome (speaking to 1 person)

tunnuq ᑐᖕᓄᑉ
fat from a land animal

tunu ᑐᓄ *back*

tunuaniittuq ᑐᓄᐊᓃᑦᑐᑉ
it's behind

tunusuk ᑐᓄᓱᑉ *nape of the neck*

tupattuq ᑐᐸᑦᑐᑉ
He/she wakes up.

tupiq ᑐᐱᑉ *tent*

tupirvik ᑐᐱᕝ
place for pitching tents

tuqtak ᑐᑉᑕᑉ *bistort (edible plant)*

tusarannaagat ᑐᓴᕋᓐᓈᒑᑦ *music*

Tusarianga quvianaqtuq.
ᑐᓴᕆᐊᖕᒐ ᖁᕕᐊᓇᖅᑐᑉ.
Happy to hear it.

tusarnirijara ᑐᓴᕐᓂᕆᔭᕋ
I like the sound of it.

tusiattuq ᑐᓯᐊᑦᑐᑉ *He/she limps.*

Tusu! ᑐᓱ! *I'm envious!*

tutsiaqtuq ᑐᑦᓯᐊᖅᑐᑉ
He/she prays.

tutsiarvik ᑐᑦᓯᐊᕝ *church*

tuttu ᑐᑦᑐ *caribou*

tuttuliaqsimava? ᑐᑦᑐᓕᐊᖅᓯᒪᕙ?
Has he gone caribou hunting.

tuttuliaqtuq ᑐᑦᑐᓕᐊᖅᑐᑉ
She / he is hunting caribou.

tuttumut anait ᑐᑦᑐᒧᑦ ᐊᓇᐃᑦ
caribou droppings

tuttumut tumiit ᑐᑦᑐᒧᑦ ᑐᒦᑦ
caribou tracks

tuttusiurvik ᑐᑦᑐᓯᐅᕐᕝ
an area where caribou are hunted

tuttuttuq ᑐᑦᑐᑦᑐᑉ
He/she caught a caribou.

tuu ᑐ *two*

tuugaalik ᑑᒑᓕᒃ *narwhal*

tuugaaq ᑑᒑᖅ *ivory*

tuumuuliqtuq ᑑᒨᓕᖅᑐᖅ.
just after 1:30 to just before 2:00

U

uamiinngaaliqtuq ᐅᐊᒦᙵᓕᖅᑐᖅ.
just after 1:00 to 1:30

uamuuqtuq ᐅᐊᒨᖅᑐᖅ.
It's 1 o'clock.

uan ᐅᐊᓐ *one*

uasikuaq ᐅᐊᓯᑯᐊᖅ *vest*

uatsiaruai ᐅᐊᑦᓯᐊᕈᐊᐃ
Just a moment.

uattiaru ᐅᐊᑦᑎᐊᕈ *later*

uattiarukkanniq ᐅᐊᑦᑎᐊᕈᒃᑲᓐᓂᖅ
in a little while

uattiaruttauq ᐅᐊᑦᑎᐊᕈᑦᑕᐅᖅ
See you in a little while.

ugguaqsimajunga ᐅᒡᒍᐊᖅᓯᒪᔪᖓ *I am regretful*

ugguarnaugaluaq
ᐅᒡᒍᐊᕐᓇᐅᒐᓗᐊᖅ
Sorry to hear it.

uik ᐅᐃᒃ *husband*

uirngaqtuq ᐅᐃᕐᖓᖅᑐᖅ
He/she sleepy.

uiviitituusuunguvit?
ᐅᐃᕖᑎᑑᓲᖑᕕᑦ?
Do you speak French?

ujamik ᐅᔭᒥᒃ *necklace*

ujaraq ᐅᔭᕋᖅ *rock*

ujjugasugiaqtuq ᐅᔾᔪᒐᓱᒋᐊᖅᑐᖅ
She / he is hunting bearded seal.

ujjuk ᐅᔾᔪᒃ *bearded seal*

ujjuttuq ᐅᔾᔪᑦᑐᖅ
He/she caught a bearded seal.

ukaliq ᐅᑲᓕᖅ *rabbit*

ukaliqtuq ᐅᑲᓕᖅᑐᖅ
He/she caught a hare.

ukalliaqtuq ᐅᑲᓪᓕᐊᖅᑐᖅ
She / he's hunting Arctic hare.

ukiaq ᐅᑭᐊᖅ *autumn*

ukiassaaq ᐅᑭᐊᔅᓵᖅ *early autumn*

ukiuq ᐅᑭᐅᖅ *winter*

Ukiuqtaqtuq ᐅᑭᐅᖅᑕᖅᑐᖅ
the Arctic

ukua ᐅᑯᐊ *these*

Ukua kisuuvat? ᐅᑯᐊ ᑭᓲᕙᑦ?
What are these?

Ukuak kisuuvaak? ᐅᑯᐊᒃ ᓯᓇᐅᕚᒃ?
What are these two things?

ulinngajuq ᐅᓕᙵᔪᖅ
It's high tide.

ulittuq ᐅᓕᑦᑐᖅ *high tide*

uliutiik ᐅᓕᐅᑏᒃ *tendon*

ullaakkut ᐅᓪᓛᒃᑯᑦ *Good Morning*

ullaaq ᐅᓪᓛᖅ *morning*

ullaktuq ᐅᓪᓚᒃᑐᖅ *He/she runs.*

ullukkut ᐅᓪᓗᒃᑯᑦ
Good Day (afternoon)

ullulimaaq ᐅᓪᓗᓕᒫᖅ *all day*

ullumi ᐅᓪᓗᒥ *today*

ulluq ᐅᓪᓗᖅ *day*

ulluqattiarit ᐅᓪᓗᖃᑦᑎᐊᕆᑦ
Have a good day (speaking to 1).

ulluriaq ᐅᓪᓗᕆᐊᖅ *star*

uluak ᐅᓗᐊᒃ *cheek (toward the ear)*

umiakkut ᐅᒥᐊᒃᑯᑦ *by boat*

umiaq ᐅᒥᐊᖅ *boat*

umiaqtuqtunga ᐅᒥᐊᖅᑐᖅᑐᖓ.
I go boating / I drive a boat.

umilik ᐅᒥᓕᒃ
a person with a beard

umimmak ᐅᒥᒻᒪᒃ *musk ox*

umimmarajak ᐅᒥᒻᒪᕋᔭᒃ
muskox wool

Umingmaktuuq ᐅᒥᖕᒪᒃᑑᖅ
Umingmaktok

una ᐅᓇ *this*

Una kisuuva? ᐅᓇ ᑭᓲᕙ?
What is this?

Una pinga. ᐅᓇ ᐱᖓ.
It's his/hers.

Una pingat. ᐅᓇ ᐱᖓᑦ. *It's theirs.*

unaaq ᐅᓈᖅ *harpoon*

ungaliagu ᐅᖓᓕᐊᒍ
the day after tomorrow

ungaliqtagit ᐅᖓᓕᖅᑕᒋᑦ
I miss you.

ungasippaa? ᐅᖓᓯᑉᐹ? *Is it far?*

ungasittuq ᐅᖓᓯᑦᑐᖅ *It's far.*

ungataaniittuq ᐅᖓᑖᓃᑦᑐᖅ
it's at the back of

unnuaq ᐅᓐᓄᐊᖅ *night*

unnuk ᐅᓐᓄᒃ *evening*

unnukkut ᐅᓐᓄᒃᑯᑦ *Good Evening*

unnuksaq ᐅᓐᓄᒃᓴᖅ *afternoon*

unnuqattiarit ᐅᓐᓄᖃᑦᑎᐊᕆᑦ
Have a good evening.

unnusakkut ᐅᓐᓄᓴᒃᑯᑦ
Good Afternoon

upalauqtuq ᐅᐸᓚᐅᖅᑐᖅ
She showed up.

upirngaaq ᐅᐱᕐᖑᖅ *spring*

uppatiik ᐅᑉᐸᑏᒃ *hips*

uppik ᐅᑉᐱᒃ *snowy owl*

uppirnangittuq ᐅᑉᐱᕐᓇᖏᑦᑐᖅ
It's amazing; unbelievable.

uqaalajuq ᐅᖃᓚᔪᖅ
She/he is phoning.

uqaalaut ᐅᖄᓚᐅᑦ
telephone

uqaalautiralaaq ᐅᖄᓚᐅᑎᕋᓛᖅ
cell phone

uqaalautisiutiit ᐅᖄᓚᐅᑎᓯᐅᑏᑦ
phone book

uqaalavigijariiqtara
ᐅᖄᓚᕕᒋᔭᕇᖅᑕᕋ
I already called him.

uqaalaviginiaqtara
ᐅᖄᓚᕕᒋᓂᐊᖅᑕᕋ
I will call him.

uqaalaviginnga ᐅᖄᓚᕕᒋᙵ
Call me.

uqakkanniruk ᐅᖃᒃᑲᓐᓂᕈᒃ
Please repeat that.

uqalimaagakkuvik ᐅᖃᓖᒪᒐᒃᑯᕕᒃ
book shelf

uqalimaagaq ᐅᖃᓖᒪᒐᖅ *book*

uqalimaaqtuq ᐅᖃᓖᒫᖅᑐᖅ
He/she reads.

uqaq ᐅᖃᖅ *tongue*

uqarajuittuq ᐅᖃᕋᔪᐃᑦᑐᖅ
He/she is very quiet.

Uqhuqtuuq ᐅᖅᓱᖅᑑᖅ *Gjoa Haven*

uqittuq ᐅᕿᑦᑐᖅ *light (weight)*

mini-dictionary : inuktitut - english

uqquujunga ᐅᖅᑰᔪᖓ *I'm hot.*

uqquujuq ᐅᖅᑰᔪᖅ *warm weather*

uqsualuk ᐅᖅᓲᐊᓗᒃ *gasoline*

uqsualuktaarvik ᐅᖅᓲᐊᓗᒃᑖᕐᕕᒃ
  gas station

uqsuaqtuq ᐅᖅᓲᐊᖅᑐᖅ
  smooth / calm seas

uqsuq ᐅᖅᓱᖅ
  fat from a sea mammal

uqsuqtirut ᐅᖅᓱᖅᑎᕈᑦ *oil*

uqumaittuq ᐅᖁᒪᐃᑦᑐᖅ *heavy*

usuk ᐅᓱᒃ *penis*

utiqtunga uvattinnut
  ᐅᑎᖅᑐᖓ ᐅᕙᑦᑎᓐᓄᑦ
  I return home.

utiqtuq ᐅᑎᖅᑐᖅ *He/she returns.*

utirumajunga ᐅᑎᕈᒪᔪᖓ
  I want to go back.

utsuuk ᐅᑦᓅᒃ *vagina*

utupiri ᐅᑐᐱᕆ *October*

uugaq ᐅᒐᖅ *cod*

uujaujaq ᐅᔪᐅᔭᖅ *green*

uujuq ᐅᔪᖅ *boiled meat*

uujuqtuqtunga ᐅᔪᖅᑐᖅᑐᖓ
  I'm eating uujuq.

uumajuq ᐅᒪᔪᖅ *animal*

uumajuqsiurvik ᐅᒪᔪᖅᓯᐅᕐᕕᒃ
  an area where wildlife is hunted

uunaqsiti ᐅᓇᖅᓯᑎ *tea kettle*

uusimajut ᐅᓯᒪᔪᑦ *cooked food*

uusimanngittut ᐅᓯᒪᙱᑦᑐᑦ
  uncooked food

uutirnaqtunga ᐅᑎᕐᓇᖅᑐᖓ
  I have a fever.

uvagut ᐅᕙᒍᑦ *we; us*

uvanga ᐅᕙᖓ *I; me*

uvaniittuq ᐅᕙᓃᑦᑐᖅ
  It's right here.

uvattinni ᐅᕙᑦᑎᓐᓂ *at my place*

uviluq ᐅᕕᓗᖅ *mussel*

uvinik ᐅᕕᓂᒃ *skin (human)*

uvininniaqtuq ᐅᕕᓂᓐᓂᐊᖅᑐᖅ
  He/she showers.

uviniruq ᐅᕕᓂᕈᖅ *t-shirt*

uvvaluunniit ᐅᕙᓘᓐᓃᑦ *or*

uvvauna ᐅᕙᐅᓇ. *It's right here.*

V

vaini ᕙᐃᓂ *wine*

vainimik ᕙᐃᓂᒥᒃ *some wine*

viivvuari ᕕᕝᕗᐊᕆ *February*

142

ᑐᑮᑦ

ᖃᓪᓗᓈᑎᑐᑦ - ᐃᓄᒃᑎᑐᑦ

mini-dictionary: english-inuktitut

A

about ᒥᑦᓵᓄᑦ mitsaanut

above (it is)
ᖁᓛᓃᑦᑐᖅ qulaaniittuq

accordion ᐃᙱᕈᑦ inngirut

adopted (were you?)
ᑎᒍᐊᖑᕖᑦ? tiguanguviit?

afraid (I am)
ᑲᑉᐱᐊᓱᒃᑐᖓ kappiasuktunga

afternoon ᐅᓐᓄᒃᓴᖅ unnuksaq

airplane ᖃᖓᑕᓲᖅ qangatasuuq

airport
ᖃᖓᑕᓲᒃᑯᕕᒃ qangatasuukkuvik

all day ᐅᓪᓗᓕᒫᖅ ullulimaaq

all week
ᐱᓇᓱᐊᕈᓯᓕᒫᖅ pinasuarusilimaaq

amauti
(long tailed) ᐊᑯᖅ akuq
(skirted) ᐊᖏᔪᖅᑕᐅᔭᖅ angijuqtaujaq

anchor ᑭᓴᐅᑦ kisaut

anchored (it is)
ᑭᓴᖅᓯᒪᔪᖅ kisaqsimajuq

and ᐊᒻᒪᓗ ammalu

angry (I am) ᓂᙵᐅᒪᔪᖓ
ninngaumajunga

animal ᐆᒪᔪᖅ uumajuq

ankle ᓯᖏᕐᓂᖅ singirniq

antler ᓇᔾᔪᒃ najjuk

apartment building
ᐃᓪᓗᐃᑦ ᐊᑕᔪᑦ illuit atajut

Apex ᓂᐊᖁᙴᑦ Niaqunnguut

appointment ᐃᓂᔅᓴᖅ inissaq

appointment (he/she makes)
ᐃᓂᔅᓴᓕᐅᖅᑐᖅ inissaliuqtuq

April ᐄᐳᕆ iipuri

Arctic
ᐅᑭᐅᖅᑕᖅᑐᖅ Ukiuqtaqtuq

Arctic Bay ᐃᒃᐱᐊᕐᔪᒃ Ikpiarjuk

arctic fox ᑎᕆᒐᓂᐊᖅ tiriganiaq

arctic ground squirrel ᓯᒃᓯᒃ siksik

arctic loon ᑲᓪᓗᓕᒃ kallulik

arctic tern ᐃᒥᖅᑯᑕᐃᓚᖅ
imiqqutailaq

arm ᑕᓕᖅ taliq

around here (it is)
ᒫᓃᑦᑐᖅ maaniittuq

around there (it is)
CDᖇᖑᑦᑐᖅ tauvaniittuq

Arviat ᐊᕐᕕᐊᑦ Arviat

August ᐊᒡᒌᓯ aaggiisi

aurora borealis
ᐊᖅᓴᕐᓃᑦ aqsarniit

autumn ᐅᑭᐊᖅ ukiaq

autumn *(early)*
ᐅᑭᐊᔅᓵᖅ ukiassaaq

B

back ᑐᓄ tunu

Baffin Island ᕿᑭᖅᑖᓗᒃ Qikiqtaaluk

bag ᐳᖅ puuq

Baker Lake
ᖃᒪᓂᑐᐊᖅ Qamani'tuaq

band *(musical)*
ᓂᕐᔫᓯᔭᖅᑎᑦ nijjausijaqtit

bank ᑭᓇᐅᔭᒃᑯᕕᒃ kiinaujakkuvik

bannock ᐸᓚᐅᒑᖅ palaugaaq

bannock (I am eating)
ᐸᓚᐅᒑᖅᑐᖅᑐᖓ
palaugaaqtuqtunga

bar ᐃᒥᕋᓚᵛᕕᒃ imiralavvik

barnacles ᑭᓕᐅᒑᐃᑦ kiliugait

baseball cap ᑎᖅᑭᐊᓕᒃ tiqqialik

Bathurst Inlet ᕿᖕᒑᐅᑦ Qingaut

bay ᑕᓯᐅᔭᖅ tasiujaq

bear
(polar) ᓇᓄᖅ nanuq
(grizzly) ᐊᒃᖤᒃ akłak

bear tracks
ᓇᓄᕐᒧᑦ ᑐᒦᑦ nanurmut tumiit

bearded seal ᐅᔾᔪᒃ ujjuk

bearded seal (he/she catches)
ᐅᔾᔪᑦᑐᖅ ujjuttuq

bearded seal (he/she hunts)
ᐅᔾᔪᒐᓱᒋᐊᖅᑐᖅ ujjugasugiaqtuq

bedroom ᐃᓪᓗᕈᓯᖅ illurusiq

beer ᐱᐊ pia

behind (it is)
ᑐᓄᐊᓃᑦᑐᖅ tunuaniittuq

belly button ᖃᓚᓯᖅ qalasiq

belt ᕿᓗᐊᖅ qiluaq

beluga ᕿᓚᓗᒑᖅ qilalugaq

beside (it is)
ᓴᓂᐊᓃᑦᑐᖅ sanianiittuq

better ᐱᐅᓂᖅᓴᖅ piuniqsaq

between (it is)
ᐊᑯᙱᓂᐊᓃᑦᑐᖅ akunninganiittuq

big ᐊᖏᔪᖅ angijuq

bill *(invoice)* ᐊᑭᓕᔅᓵᖅ akilissaq

birds ᑎᒻᒥᐊᑦ timmiat

bistort *(edible plant)* ᑐᖅᑕᒃ tuqtak

bit *(a little)* ᒥᑭᔪᒥᒃ. mikijumik

black ᕿᕐᓂᖅᑐᖅ qirniqtuq

black guillemot
ᐱᑦᑎᐅᓛᖅ pittiulaaq

bleeding (I am)
ᐊᐅᓈᖅᑐᖓ. aunaaqtunga

blizzarding (it is)
ᐱᖅᓯᖅᑐᖅ piqsiqtuq

blood ᐊᐅᒃ auk

blouse ᑭᐊᑎ kiati

blue ᑐᖑᔪᖅᑐᖅ tungujuqtuq

blueberry
ᑭᒍᑕᖏᕐᓇᖅ kigutangirnaq

boardroom
ᑲᑎᒪᕕᒃ katimavik

boat ᐅᒥᐊᖅ umiaq

boating (I go)
ᐅᒥᐊᖅᑐᖅᑐᖓ umiaqtuqtunga

body ᑎᒥ timi

book ᐅᖃᓕᒫᒐᖅ uqalimaagaq

book shelf
ᐅᖃᓕᒫᒐᒃᑯᕕᒃ uqalimaagakkuvik

boots
(skin) ᑲᒦᒃ kamiik
(rubber) ᑲᒫᓘᒃ kamaaluuk
(long) ᑲᒥᑯᑖᒃ kamikutaak
(winter) ᑲᒫᓘᒃ ᐅᑭᐅᖅᓯᐅᑏᒃ
kamaaluuk ukiuqsiutii

bow *(of a boat)* ᓯᕗᐊ sivua

bowhead whale ᐊᕐᕕᒃ arvik

bracelet ᑕᓕᐊᙳᐊᖅ taliannguaq

breasts ᐃᕕᐊᖐᒃ iviangiik

broken (it is) ᓱᕋᑦᑐᖅ surattuq

broth ᖃᔪᖅ qajuq

brother of a female ᐊᓂᒃ anik

brow ᕿᙳᖅ qinnguq

brown ᑲᔪᖅ kajuq

bullets ᓴᒃᑯᑦ sakkut

busy (I am very)
ᐱᔭᔅᓴᖃᓗᐊᖅᑐᖓ
pijassaqaluaqtunga

but ᑭᓯᐊᓂ kisiani

buttock ᓄᓗ nulu

button ᐃᓯᕆᐅᑦ isiriut

buys (he/she)
ᓂᐅᕕᖅᑐᖅ niuviqtuq

C

cabin ᐃᓪᓗᕋᓛᖅ illuralaaq

calls (she/he) ᐅᖄᓚᔪᖅ uqaalajuq

Cambridge Bay
ᐃᖃᓗᒃᑑᑦᑎᐊᖅ Iqaluktuuttiaq

camp stove ᓲᐴᔪᖅ supuujuq

Canada goose ᓂᕐᓕᒃ nirlik

Canadian Broadcasting Corp (CBC)
ᓰᐲᓰᒃᑯᑦ Siipiisiikkut

candle ᐸᑎᐅᔭᖅ patiujaq

cap *(baseball)* ᑎᖅᑭᐊᓕᒃ tiqqialik

Cape Dorset ᑭᙵᐃᑦ Kinngait

cards (I play)
ᒪᑭᑦᑕᖅᑐᖓ makittaqtunga

caribou ᑐᑦᑐ tuttu

caribou (he/she catches)
ᑐᑦᑐᑦᑐᖅ tuttuttuq

caribou (he/she hunts)
ᑐᑦᑐᓕᐊᖅᑐᖅ tuttuliaqtuq

caribou droppings
ᑐᑦᑐᒧᑦ ᐊᓇᐃᑦ tuttumut anait

caribou fat *(boiled & hardened)*
ᐳᓐᓂᕐᓂᖅ punnirniq

caribou skin ᐊᒥᖅ amiq

caribou tracks
ᑐᑦᑐᒧᑦ ᑐᒦᑦ tuttumut tumiit

carving ᓴᓇᙳᐊᒐᖅ sanannguagaq

CD (compact disk)
ᕿᓪᓕᖅᑐᖅ qilliqtuq

cell phone
ᐅᖄᓚᐅᑎᕋᓛᖅ uqaalautiralaaq

char ᐃᖃᓗᒃ iqaluk

cheap ᐊᑭᑭᑦᑐᖅ akikittuq

cheek
(by the nose) ᐃᖅᓴᖅ iqsaq
(toward the ear) ᐅᓗᐊᒃ uluak

chest ᓴᕝᕕᒃ savvik

Chesterfield Inlet
ᐃᒡᓗᓕᒑᕐᔪᒃ Igluligaarjuk

child *(one's own)*
ᕿᑐᕐᖓᖅ qiturngaq

church ᑐᑦᓯᐊᕐᕕᒃ tutsiarvik

cigarettes ᓯᒡᒐᓕᐊᑦ siggaliat

cinema ᑕᕐᕆᔭᕐᕕᒃ tarrijarvik

clam ᐊᒻᒨᒪᔪᖅ ammuumajuq

cleaning up (I am)
ᐱᕈᓇᖅᓴᖅᑐᖓ pirunaqsaqtunga

clear skies ᓯᓚᖅᑭᖅᑐᖅ silaqqiqtuq

cliff ᐃᓐᓈᕈᖅ innaaruq

close *(distance)* ᖃᓂᑦᑐᖅ qanittuq

close (it is)
ᖃᓂᑦᑐᕈᓗᒃ qanitturuluk

closed (it is)
ᒪᑐᓯᒪᔪᖅ matusimajuq

clothing ᐊᓐᓄᕌᑦ annuraat

cloud ᓄᕗᔭ nuvuja

cloudberry ᐊᖅᐱᒃ aqpik

cloudy (it is) ᓄᕗᔭᔪᖅ nuvujajuq

Clyde River
ᑲᖏᖅᑐᒑᐱᒃ Kangiqtugaapik

cod ᐆᒐᖅ uugaq

coffee ᑳᐱ kaapi

coffee (I am drinking)
ᑳᐱᑐᖅᑐᖓ kaapituqtunga

coffee shop ᑳᐱᑐᕐᕕᒃ kaapiturvik

cold (I am) ᕿᐅᔪᖓ qiujunga

cold (I have a)
ᓄᕙᑦᑐᖓ nuvattunga

cold weather
ᓂᓪᓚᓱᒃᑐᖅ nillasuktuq

colours ᐊᒥᐊᑦ amiat

common law *(spouse)*
ᐊᐃᑉᐸᖅ aippaq

community ᓄᓇᓕᒃ nunalik

computer ᖃᕋᓴᐅᔭᖅ qarasaujaq

cooked (food) ᐆᓯᒪᔪᑦ uusimajut

cookie ᓯᕙᐅᔭᖅ sivaujaq

cooking (I am)
ᓂᖅᑎᐅᖅᑐᖓ niqtiuqtunga

Coral Harbour ᓴᓪᓖᑦ Salliit

corner store
ᓂᐅᕕᕐᕕᕋᓛᖅ niuvirviralaaq

cost ᐊᑭᖓ akinga

coughing (I am)
ᖁᐃᖅᓱᖅᑐᖓ quiqsuqtunga

courthouse
ᐃᖅᑲᖅᑐᐃᕕᒃ iqqaqtuivik

cranberry ᑭᒻᒥᓐᓇᖅ kimminnaq

creek ᑰᒐᓛᒃ kuugalaak

crew *(aircraft)* ᐱᔨᑲᑖᑦ pijikataat

cross-bar *(qamutiik)* ᓇᐳ napu

crowberry ᐸᐅᕐᖓᖅ paurngaq

cry (he/she) ᕿᐊᔪᖅ qiaqqaujunga

cup ᐃᕐᖑᓯᖅ irngusiq

curly hair ᐃᕿᓱᓕᒃ iqisulik

D

dances (he/she)
ᒧᒥᖅᑐᖅ mumiqtuq

dancing (I go)
ᒧᒥᕆᐊᖅᑐᖓ mumiriaqtunga

daughter ᐸᓂᒃ panik

day ᐅᓪᓗᖅ ulluq

day after tomorrow
ᐅᖓᓕᐊᒍ ungaliagu

day before yesterday
ᐃᑉᐸᑦᓵᓂ ippassaani

daycare ᐸᐃᕆᕕᒃ pairivik

December ᑎᓯᐱᕆ tisipiri

dentist's office
ᑭᒍᓐᓂᐊᕐᕕᒃ kigunniarvik

Department of Education
ᐃᓕᓐᓂᐊᖅᑐᓕᕆᔨᒃᑯᑦ
Ilinniaqtulirijikkut

Department of Justice
ᒪᓕᒐᓕᕆᔨᒃᑯᑦ Maligalirijikkut

different (they are)
ᐊᑦᔨᒌᓐᖏᑦᑑᒃ ajjigiinngittuuk

dining room ᓂᕆᕕᒃ nirivik

director *(job title)*
ᑐᑭᒨᐊᑦᑎᓯᔨ tukimuatitsiji

document ᑎᑎᖅᑲᖅ titiqqaq

dog ᕿᒻᒥᖅ qimmiq

dog *(lead of a team)*
ᐃᓱᕋᖅᑐᔪᖅ isuraqtujuq

dog harness ᐊᓄ anu

dog team ᕿᒧᑦᓯᑦ qimussit

dog traces ᐃᐱᐅᑦ ipiutat

dog whip ᐃᐸᕋᐅᑦ iparaut

done (I am)
ᐱᔭᕇᖅᑐᖓ pijariiqtunga

door ᒪᑐ; ᐹ matu; paa

down there (it is)
ᑕᐅᓇᓃᑦᑐᖅ taunaniittuq

dreaming (I am)
ᓯᓐᓇᑐᖅᑐᖓ sinnatuqtunga

dress ᐊᑕᔪᖅ atajuq

dried fish ᐱᑦᑎ pitti

dried meat ᓂᒃᑯᒃ nikkuk

drive a boat (he/she)
ᐅᒥᐊᖅᑐᖅᑐᖅ umiaqtuqtuq

drives a car (he/she)
ᓄᓇᓯᐅᖅᑐᖅ nunasiuqtuq

drives a snowmobile (he/she)
ᖃᒧᑕᐅᔭᖅᑐᖅ qamutaujaqtuq

drizzling (it is) ᒥᓂᔪᖅ minijuq

drums ᐊᓇᐅᓪᓚᒐᑦ anaullagat

dry ᐸᓂᖅᑐᖅ paniqtuq

duck ᒥᑎᖅ mitiq

E

ear ᓯᐅᑦ siut

earrings ᓯᐅᒻᒥᐅᑖᒃ siummiutaak

eating (I am) ᓂᕆᔪᖓ nirijunga

eel ᖁᔾᔭᐅᓐᓇᑦ qujjaunnat

eggs ᒪᓐᓃᑦ manniit

eight ᐃᑦ iit

eight *(traditional)*
ᓯᑕᒪᐅᔪᖅᑐᑦ sitamaujuqtut

elbow ᐃᑯᓯᒃ ikusik

electrician
ᓄᑭᓪᓚᐅᓯᕆᔨ nukillausiriji

eleven ᐃᓕᐊᐸᓐ iliapan

email ᐃᕐᖏᓇᐊᖅᑕᐅᑦ irngiinaaqtaut

entering (I am) ᐃᓯᖅᑐᖓ isiqtunga

entrance way ᐹ paa

envious (I am) ᑐᓱ! Tusu!

environment ᓯᓚ sila

evening ᐅᓐᓄᒃ unnuk

exercises (he/she)
ᐃᖃᐃᓕᓴᖅᑐᖅ iqailisaqtuq

expensive ᐊᑭᑐᔪᖅ akitujuq

eye ᐃᔨ iji

eyebrow ᖃᓪᓗ qallu

eyelashes ᕿᒥᕆᐊᑦ qimiriat

F

face ᑮᓇᖅ kiinaq

family ᐃᓚᒌᑦ ilagiit

far ᐅᖓᓯᑦᑐᖅ ungasittuq

fast ᓱᒃᑲᔪᖅ sukkajuq

fat from a land animal
ᑐᓐᓄᖅ tunnuq

fat from a sea mammal
ᐅᖅᓱᖅ uqsuq

father ᐊᑖᑕ ataata

fax machine
ᓱᒃᑲᔪᒃᑰᕈᑦ sukkajukkuurut

feast *(community event)*
ᓂᕆᕖᔾᔪᐊᖅ nirivijjuaq

February
ᕖᕝᕗᐊᕆ viivvuari

fermented walrus meat
ᐃᒍᓇᖅ igunaq

fever (I have a)
ᐆᑎᕐᓇᖅᑐᖓ uutirnaqtunga

few ᐊᒥᓲᙱᑦᑐᑦ amisuunngittut

fine (he/she is)
ᖃᓄᐃᙱᑦᑐᖅ qanuinngittuq

finger *(index)* ᑎᑭᖅ tikiq

fiord ᑲᖏᖅᑐᒃ kangiqtuk

fire hall ᖃᑦᑎᕆᔨᒃᑯᑦ qattirijikkut

firefighter ᖃᑦᑎᕆᔨ qattiriji

first floor
ᖁᓛ ᓯᕗᓪᓕᖅ qulaa sivulliq

first one
ᓯᕗᓪᓕᖅᐹᖅ sivulliqpaaq

fish ᐃᖃᓗᒃ iqaluk

fish store
ᐃᖃᓗᒃᑖᕐᕕᒃ iqaluktaarvik

fishing (I go)
ᐃᖃᓪᓕᐊᖅᑐᖓ iqalliaqtunga

five ᑕᓪᓕᒪᑦ tallimat

five *(borrowed from English)*
ᐸᐃ pai

flowers ᓄᓇᕋᐃᑦ nunarait

foggy (it is) ᑕᑦᓯᖅᑐᖅ tatsiqtuq

food (cooked) ᐆᓯᒪᔪᑦ uusimajut

food (uncooked)
ᐆᓯᒪᖏᑦᑐᑦ uusimangittut

foot ᐃᓯᒐᒃ isigak

forearm ᐊᒡᒐᐅᑦ aggaut

forehead ᖃᐅᖅ qauq

fork ᑲᑭᐊᒃ kakiak

four
ᓯᑕᒪᑦ / ᑎᓴᒪᑦ sitamat / tisamat

four *(borrowed from English)*
ᐳᐊ pua

fox ᑎᕆᒐᓂᐊᖅ tiriganiaq

fox fur
ᑎᕆᒐᓂᐊᕋᔭᒃ tiriganiarajak

freezer ᖁᐊᒃᑯᕕᒃ quakkuvik

Friday ᑕᓪᓕᕐᒥᖅ tallirmiq

fridge ᖁᐊᖃᐅᑦ quaqaut

front of (it is in)
ᓵᖓᓃᑦᑐᖅ saanganiittuq

frostbite (you have)
ᕿᕿᓯᒪᔪᑎᑦ qiqisimajutit

frying pan ᓵᑦᑑᔭᐅᑦ saattuujaut

full (I am)
ᐊᕿᐊᑦᑐᖅᑐᖓ aqiattuqtunga

fur
(fox) ᑎᕆᒐᓂᐊᕋᔭᒃ tiriganiarajak
(polar bear) ᓇᓄᕋᖅ nanuraq

G

game ᐱᙵᐊᖅ pinnguaq

gas can ᐸᐃᒡᒑᓚ paiggaala

gas station
ᐅᖅᓱᐊᓗᒃᑖᕐᕕᒃ uqsualuktaarvik

gasoline ᐅᖅᓱᐊᓗᒃ uqsualuk

Get in / on *(command)*
ᐃᑭᒋᑦ ikigit

Get off *(command)*
ᓂᐅᒋᑦ niugit

Gjoa Haven ᐅᖅᓱᖅᑑᖅ Uqhuqtuuq

glacier ᐊᐅᔪᐃᑦᑐᖅ aujuittuq

gloves ᐊᒡᒑᒃ aggaak

gold ᒎᓗ guulu

good ᐱᐅᔪᖅ piujuq

Good Afternoon
ᐅᓐᓄᓴᒃᑯᑦ unnusakkut

Good Day *(afternoon)*
ᐅᓪᓗᒃᑯᑦ ullukkut

Good Evening ᐅᓐᓄᒃᑯᑦ unnukkut

Good Morning ᐅᓪᓛᒃᑯᑦ ullaakkut

Good to hear that.
ᐊᓱᑯᓗᒃ asukuluk

good weather
ᓯᓚᑦᑎᐊᕙᒃ silattiavak

Good-bye
(to 1) ᑕᕝᕙᐅᕗᑎᑦ tavvauvutit
(to 2) ᑕᕝᕙᐅᕗᓯᒃ tavvauvusik
(to 3+) ᑕᕝᕙᐅᕗᓯ tavvauvusi

GPS ᑕᒻᒪᕇᒃᑯᑦ tammariikkut

grandchild ᐃᕐᖑᑕᖅ irngutaq

grandfather
ᐊᑖᑕᑦᓯᐊᖅ; ᐃᑦᑐᖅ
ataatatsiaq; ittuq

grandmother
ᐊᓈᓇᑦᓯᐊᖅ; ᓂᖏᐅᖅ
anaanatsiaq; ningiuq

green ᐆᔭᐅᔭᖅ uujaujaq

Greenland ᐊᑯᑭᑦᑐᖅ Akukittuq

grey ᓯᐊᕐᓇᖅ siarnaq

Grise Fiord ᐊᐅᓱᐃᑦᑐᖅ Ausuittuq

grizzly bear ᐊᒃᖠᒃ akłak

guitar ᑯᒃᑭᑦᑕᐹᕈᑦ kukkittapaarut

gun ᐃᓪᓗᐃᓇᖅᑑᑦ illuinaqtuut

H

hair
(general) ᓄᔭᑦ nujat
(curly) ᐃᕿᓱᓕᒃ iqisulik
(long) ᓄᔭᑯᑖᒃ nujakutaak
(short) ᓄᔭᑭᑦᑐᖅ nujakittuq
(white) ᖀᖅ qiiq

Hall Beach ᓴᓂᕋᔭᒃ Sanirajak

hamlet office
Hᐋᒪᓚᒃᑯᑦ Haamalakkut

hand ᐊᒡᒐᒃ aggak

harbour seal ᖃᓯᒋᐊᖅ qasigiaq

hard ∩ᒷᐦᔭᖅ tisijuq

hare (he/she catches)
ᐅᑲᖦᖅᑐᖅ ukaliqtuq

hare (he/she hunts)
ᐅᑲᖦᖤᐊᖅᑐᖅ ukalliaqtuq

harp seal ᖃᐃᕈᓕᒃ qairulik

harpoon ᐅᓈᖅ unaaq

hat ᓇᓴᖅ nasaq

head ᓂᐊᖁᖅ niaquq

head (top of the) ᑲᔾᔨᖅ kajjiq

headache (I have a)
ᓂᐊᖁᙲᔪᙵ niaqunngujunga

heavy ᐅᖁᒪᐃᑦᑐᖅ uqumaittuq

heel ᑭᒻᒥᒃ kimmik

here (it is) ᒫᓃᑦᑐᖅ maaniittuq

hers (it is) ᐅᓇ ᐱᖓ. Una pinga.

high tide ᐅᓕᑦᑐᖅ ulittuq

high tide (it is)
ᐅᓕᙱᒪᔪᖅ ulinngajuq

highlands ᐳᖅᑐᔪᑦ puqtujut

hill ᖃᖅᖃᔮᖅ qaqqajaaq

hips ᐅᑉᐸᑏᒃ uppatiik

his (it is) ᐅᓇ ᐱᖓ. Una pinga.

hitch ᑲᓗᑎ kaluti

hockey (I play)
ᕼᐊᑭᖅᑐᙵ haakiqtunga

hockey arena
ᕼᐊᑭᕐᕕᒃ hakirvik

home (I am going)
ᐊᙱᕋᖅᓕᖅᑐᙵ angirraliqtunga

hooded seal ᓇᑦᑎᕙᒃ nattivak

hospital ᐋᓐᓂᐊᕕᒃ aanniavik

hot (I am) ᐅᖅᑯᔪᙵ uqquujunga

hotel ᑐᔪᕐᒥᕕᒃ tujurmivik

house ᐃᒡᓗ illu

how? ᖃᓄᖅ? qanuq?

hungry (I am) ᑳᒃᑐᙵ kaaktunga

hunting ᐊᖑᓇᓱᒃᑐᖅ angunasuktuq

Hurry up! ᑐᐊᕕᓚᐅᕆᑦ! Tuavilaurit!

hurting (it is) ᒪᐃᑦᑐᖅ maittuq

husband ᐅᐃᒃ uik

I

I ᐅᕙᙵ uvanga

ice ᓯᑯ siku

ice fog (there is) ᐸᑐᑦᑐᖅ patuttuq

Igloolik ᐃᒡᓗᓕᒃ Iglulik

index finger ᑎᑭᖅ tikiq

infected (it is) ᐃᒻᒪᑦᑐᖅ immattuq

inlet ᑲᙱᖅᑐᒃ kangiqtuk

inside ᐃᓗᐊᓂ iluani

inside (it is) ᐃᓗᐊᓃᑦᑐᖅ iluaniittuq

Inuktitut (I speak)
ᐃᓄᒃᑎᑑᓲᖑᔪᙵ
inuktituusuungujunga

island ᕿᑭᖅᑕᖅ qikiqtaq

ivory ᑑᒑᖅ tuugaaq

J

jacket ᔭᐃᑲᒃ jaikak

jam ᔮ jaa

January ᔮᓐᓄᐊᕆ jaannuari

150

jewelry
ᑕᑯᒥᓇᖅᓴᐅᑎᑦ takuminaqsautit

July ᔪᓚᐃ julai

jumps (he/she)
ᕿᒡᒋᖅᑕᖅᑐᖅ qiggiqtaqtuq

June ᔫᓂ juuni

K

kamotik ᖃᒧᑏᒃ qamutiik

kayak ᖃᔭᖅ qajaq

kayak paddle ᐸᐅᑏᒃ pautiik

kettle ᐆᓇᖅᓯᑏᑦ uunaqsitiit

keyboard ᓇᖅᑉᑕᐅᑦ naqittaut

Kimmirut ᐱᒻᒥᕈᑦ Kimmirut

kitchen ᑰᖅᒐᕐᕕᒃ kuuqarvik

Kitikmeot Region
ᕿᑎᕐᒥᐅᑦ Qitirmiut

knapsack ᓇᒻᒪᒑᖅ nammagaaq

knee ᓰᖅᑯᖅ siiqquq

knife ᓴᕕᒃ savik

Kugaaruk ᑰᒑᕐᔪᒃ Kuugaarjuk

Kugluktuk ᖁᓗᖅᑐᖅ Qurluqtuq

L

Labrador ᓄᓇᑦᓯᐊᕗᑦ Nunatsiavut

lake ᑕᓯᖅ tasiq

lamp ᖃᐅᒻᒪᖅᑯᑦ qaummaqqut

land ᓄᓇ nuna

lands a boat (he) ᑐᓚᑦᑐᖅ tulattuq

laptop
ᖃᕋᓴᐅᔭᕋᓛᖅ qarasaujaralaaq

last month
ᑕᖅᑭᐅᓚᐅᖅᑐᖅ taqqiulauqtuq

last one
ᑭᖑᓪᓕᖅᐹᖅ kingulliqpaaq

last week
ᐱᓇᓱᐊᕈᓯᐅᓚᐅᖅᑐᖅ
pinasuarusiulauqtuq

last year ᐊᕐᕌᓂ arraani

later ᐅᐊᑦᑎᐊᕈ uattiaru

launches a boat (he)
ᓵᕕᑦᑐᖅ saavittuq

lead dog (dog team)
ᐃᓱᕋᖅᑐᔪᖅ isuraqtujuq

leaving (I am) ᐊᓂᔪᖓ anijunga

left ᓴᐅᒥᒃ saumik

leg ᓂᐅ niu

lemming ᐊᕕᙵᖅ avinngaq

light (weight) ᐅᕿᑦᑐᖅ uqittuq

lighter *(cigarette)*
ᐃᓐᓈᖅ; ᑲᓱᒃ innaq; kasuk

limping (I am)
ᑐᓯᐊᑦᑐᖓ tusiattunga

lip ᖃᖅᑐ qaqtu

living room ᐳᓛᕐᕕᒃ pulaarvik

long hair ᓄᔭᑯᑖᒃ nujakutaak

loon ᑲᓪᓗᓕᒃ kallulik

love (I...him/her)
ᓇᓪᓕᒋᔭᕋ nalligijara

love (I...you)
ᓇᓪᓕᒋᕙᒋᑦ nalligivagit

low tide (it is)
ᑎᓂᙵᔪᖅ tininngajuq

luggage ᐃᑦᑎᕐᕕᒃ ittirvik

M

mainland ᐃᓗᐃᓕᖅ iluiliq

many ᐊᒥᓱᑦ amisut

March ᒫᑦᓯ maatsi

matches ᐃᑯᒪᑦ ikumat

May ᒪᐃ mai

maybe ᐃᒻᒪᖃ immaqa

me ᐅᕙᖓ uvanga

meat
(boiled) ᐆᔪᖅ uujuq
(frozen) ᖁᐊᖅ quaq
(raw) ᒥᑭᒐᖅ mikigaq
(with bones) ᑭᒃᑲᔮᖅ kikkajaaq

meeting (they are)
ᑲᑎᒪᔪᑦ katimajut

milk ᐃᒻᒧᒃ immuk

mine (it is) ᐱᒐ piga

minke whale ᑎᑳᒍᓪᓕᒃ tikaagullik

miss (I...you)
ᐅᖓᓕᖅᑕᒋᑦ ungaliqtagit

mittens ᐳᐊᓘᒃ pualuuk

Monday ᓇᒡᒐᔾᔭᐅ naggajjau

money ᑮᓇᐅᔭᖅ kiinaujaq

month ᑕᖅᑭᖅ taqqiq

montitor *(computer)*
ᐃᒐᓛᖑᔭᖅ igalaangujaq

moon ᑕᖅᑭᖅ taqqiq

morning ᐅᓪᓛᖅ ullaaq

mother ᐊᓈᓇ anaana

motor *(outboard)*
ᐊᐅᓚᐅᑎᑦ aulautit

mountain ᖃᖅᑲᖅ qaqqaq

mountains ᑭᙵᐃᑦ kinngait

mouse *(computer)*
ᐊᕕᙵᙳᐊᖅ avinngannguaq

mouth ᖃᓂᖅ qaniq

mud ᒪᕐᕋᖅ marraq

muktuk *(skin of a whale that is eaten)*
ᒪᑦᑖᖅ mattaaq

murre ᐊᒃᐸ akpa

museum
ᑕᑯᔭᒐᖃᕐᕕᒃ takujagaqarvik

music
ᓂᔾᔮᔪᑦ / ᑐᓴᕐᓈᒐᑦ
nijjaajut / tusarannaagat

musicians
ᓂᔾᔭᐅᓯᔭᖅᑎᑦ nijjausijaqtit

musk ox ᐅᒥᒻᒪᒃ umimmak

muskox wool
ᐅᒥᒻᒪᕋᔭᒃ umimmarajak

mussel ᐅᕕᓗᖅ uviluq

N

nape of the neck ᑐᓄᓱᒃ tunusuk

narrows *(ocean passage)*
ᐃᑭᖅ ikiq

narwhal ᑑᒑᓕᒃ tuugaalik

nauseous (I feel)
ᒥᕆᐊᙳᔪᖓ mirianngujunga

near ᖃᓂᑦᑐᖅ qanittuq

neck ᖁᖓᓯᖅ qungasiq

necklace ᐅᔭᒥᒃ ujamik

next month
ᑕᖅᑭᐅᓛᖅᑐᖅ taqqiulaaqtuq

next week
ᐱᓇᓱᐊᕈᓯᐅᓛᖅᑐᖅ
pinasuarusiulaaqtuq

next year ᐊᕐᕌᒍ arraagu

night ᐅᓄᐊᖅ unnuaq

nine ᓇᐃᓐ nain

nine *(traditional)*
ᖁᓕᐅᕐᙵᒋᐊᖅᑐᑦ quliunngigaqtut

no
(N. Baffin) ᐋᒃᑲ aakka
(S. Baffin) ᐋᒡᒐ aagga

noon ᖁᓛᓂ qulaani

northern lights ᐊᖅᓴᕐᓃᑦ aqsarniit

Northwest Territories
ᓄᓇᑦᓯᐊᖅ Nunatsiaq

nose ᕿᖓᖅ qingaq

not yet ᐋᒡᒐ ᓱᓕ aagga suli

November ᓄᕕᐱᕆ nuvipiri

now ᒫᓐᓇ maanna

number ᓈᓴᐅᑎ naasauti

Nunavik ᓄᓇᕕᒃ Nunavik

nursing station
ᐋᓐᓂᐊᕕᒃ aanniavik

O

O.K. (it is) ᓈᒻᒪᑦᑐᖅ naammattuq

oar ᐃᐳᑦ ipuut

October ᐅᑐᐱᕆ utupiri

off (it is) ᖃᒥᓐᖓᔪᖅ qaminngajuq

office ᐊᓪᓚᕕᒃ allavvik

oil ᐅᖅᓱᖅᑎᕈᑦ uqsuqtirut

on (it is) ᐃᑯᒪᔪᖅ ikumajuq

one ᐊᑕᐅᓯᖅ atausiq

one *(borrowed from English)*
ᐅᐊᓐ uan

open (it is) ᒪᑐᐃᖕᒐᔪᖅ matuingajuq

or ᐅᕝᕙᓘᓐᓃᑦ uvvaluunniit

orange ᐊᐅᐸᔮᖕᒐᔪᖅ aupajaangajuq

outboard motor
ᐊᐅᓚᐅᑎᑦ aulautit

outdoors (the) ᓯᓚ sila

outside ᓯᓚᒥ silami

over there (it is)
ᑕᐃᑲᓃᑦᑐᖅ taikaniittuq

owl (snowy) ᐅᑉᐱᒃ uppik

P

paid ᐊᑭᓕᖅᑐᖅ akiliqtuq

pair ᐃᓪᓗᒌᒃ illugiik

pair (one of a)
ᐃᒡᓗᐃᓐᓇᖅ igluinnaq

palm of the hand ᐃᑎᒪᒃ itimak

Pangnirtung ᐸᙱᖅᑑᖅ Panniqtuuq

pants
(general) ᖃᕐᓖᒃ qarliik
(skin) ᖃᕐᓕᑲᓪᓛᒃ qarlikallaak
(wind) ᖃᕐᓕᐊᓘᒃ qarlialuuk

paper ᐸᐃᑉᐹᖅ paippaaq

park ᒥᕐᙳᐃᖅᓯᕐᕕᒃ mirnguiqsirvik

parka
(contemporary)
ᖁᓕᑦᑕᐅᔭᖅ qulittaujaq

(traditional, fur on inside)
ᐊᑎᒋ atigi

(traditional, fur on outside)
ᖁᓕᑦᑕᖅ qulittaq

(with pouch for carrying a child)
ᐊᒪᐅᑎ amauti

(outer shell)
ᓯᓚᐹᖅ silapaaq

partner *(spouse)*
ᐊᐃᑉᐸᖅ aippaq

pen ᑎᑎᕋᐅᑦ titiraut

pencil ᑎᑎᕋᐅᑦ titiraut

penis ᐅᓱᒃ usuk

pharmacy
ᐄᔭᒐᖅᑖᕐᕕᒃ iijagaqtaarvik

phone book
ᐅᖃᓛᐅᑎᓯᐅᑏᑦ uqaalautisiutiit

phones (he/she)
ᐅᖃᓛᔪᖅ uqaalajuq

photocopier
ᐊᒥᓱᓕᐅᕈᑦ amisuliurut

piano ᐱᐊᓇ piana

pill ᐄᔭᒐᖅ iijagaq

pilot
ᐊᖁᑏ; ᖃᖓᑕᓲᖅᑎ
aquti; qangatasuuqti

plants ᐱᕈᖅᑐᑦ piruqtut

plate ᐸᓕᐊᖅ paliaq

plays a game (he/she)
ᐱᙳᐊᖅᑐᖅ pinnguaqtuq

plays music (he/she)
ᓂᔾᔮᐅᓯᔭᖅᑐᖅ nijjausijaqtuq

pleasant *(time or place)*
ᑲᔾᔮᓇᖅᑐᖅ kajjaanaqtuq

pocket ᐃᑉᐱᐊᕐᔪᒃ ippiarjuk

point ᓄᕗᐊ nuvua

polar bear ᓇᓄᖅ nanuq

polar bear (he/she hunts)
ᓇᓐᓂᐊᖅᑐᖅ nanniaqtuq

polar bear fur ᓇᓄᕋᖅ nanuraq

police ᐸᓖᓯ paliisi

police department
ᐸᓖᓯᒃᑯᑦ paliisikkut

pond ᑕᓯᐊᕐᔪᒃ tasiarjuk

Pond Inlet ᒥᑦᑎᒪᑕᓕᒃ Mittimatalik

possibly ᐄᖃᐃ iiqai

post office
ᑎᑎᖅᑲᓂᐊᕐᕕᒃ titiqqaniarvik

prays (he / she)
ᑐᑦᓯᐊᖅᑐᖅ tutsiaqtuq

prepares to depart (he/she)
ᐸᕐᓇᑦᑐᖅ parnattuq

price ᐊᑭᖓ akinga

print ᑎᑎᖅᑐᒐᖅ titiqtugaq

printer
ᐸᐃᑉᐹᒨᕆᔾᔪᑦ paippaamuurijjut

ptarmigan ᐊᕐᕕᒡᒋᖅ aqiggiq

ptarmigan droppings
ᐊᕐᕕᒡᒋᒧᑦ ᐊᓇᐃᑦ aqiggimut anait

ptarmigan tracks ᐊᕐᕕᒡᒋᒧᑦ ᑐᒦᑦ
aqiggimut tumiit

purple ᐃᑦᑎᙳᐊᖅ ittinnguaq

Q

qamutiik runners ᐱᕐᕌᒃ pirraak

Qikiqtarjuaq (Broughton Island)
ᕿᑭᖅᑕᕐᔪᐊᖅ Qikiqtarjuaq

R

rabbit ᐅᑲᓕᖅ ukaliq

radio ᓈᓚᐅᑦ naalaut

radio station
ᓈᓚᐅᑎᖃᕐᕕᒃ naalautiqarvik

rains (it)
ᓯᓚᓗᑦᑐᖅ; ᒪᑯᖅᑐᖅ
silaluttuq; makuqtuq

Rankin Inlet
ᑲᖏᖅᖠᓂᖅ Kangiqłiniq

raw meat ᒥᑭᒐᖅ mikigaq

reading (I am)
ᐅᖃᓕᒫᖅᑐᖓ uqalimaaqtunga

ready (it is)
ᐱᔭᕇᖅᓯᒪᔪᖅ pijariiqsimajuq

recreational centre
ᐱᙳᐊᕐᕕᒃ pinnguarvik

red ᐊᐅᐸᖅᑐᖅ aupaqtuq

regretful (I am)
ᐅᒡᒍᐊᖅᓯᒪᔪᖓ ugguaqsimajunga

Repulse Bay ᓇᐅᔮᑦ Naujaat

Resolute Bay
ᖃᐅᓯᐅᑦᑐᖅ Qausuittuq

restaurant ᓂᕆᕕᒃ nirivik

ribs ᑐᓕᒫᑦ tulimaat

rifle ᖁᑭᐅᑦ qukiut

right ᑕᓕᖅᐱᒃ taliqpik

ring
ᓇᒡᒍᐊᕐᒥᒃ; ᐊᒡᒑᒻᒥᒃ
nagguarmik; aggammik

ringed seal ᓇᑦᑎᖅ nattiq

ringed seal (he/she catches)
ᓇᑦᑎᖅᑐᖅ nattiqtuq

river ᑰᒃ kuuk

rock ᐅᔭᕋᖅ ujaraq

rocks *(for securing a tent)*
ᐱᕈᑦ pirut

rocky ground
ᖃᐃᖅᓱᒑᖅ qaiqsugaaq

rope ᐊᑦᑐᓈᖅ attunaaq

ropes (*for securing a tent)*
ᓄᖃᕈᑎᑦ nuqarutit

row house ᐃᓪᓗᑯᑖᑦ illukutaat

rubber boots ᑲᒫᓘᒃ kamaaluuk

runners *(qamutiik)* ᐲᕐᒑᒃ piraak

runs (he/she) ᐅᓪᓚᒃᑐᖅ ullaktuq

S

sad (I am) ᖁᓱᔪᖓ qusujunga

salt ᑕᕆᐅᖅ tariuq

same (they are the) ᐊᔾᔨᒌᒃ ajjigiik

sand ᓯᐅᕋᖅ siuraq

Saturday ᓯᕙᑖᕐᕕᒃ sivataarvik

scallop ᑕᓪᓗᕈᓐᓇᖅ tallurunnaq

scarf ᖁᖓᓯᕈᖅ qungasiruq

scarf *(kercheif)* ᓇᓴᕈᕚᖅ nasaruvaaq

school ᐃᓕᓐᓂᐊᕐᕕᒃ ilinniarvik

scissors ᐊᓪᓕᕈᔮᒃ allirujaak

scope ᕿᙳᑦ qinngut

screen *(computer)*
ᐃᒐᓛᖑᔭᖅ igalaangujaq

sculpin ᑲᓇᔪᖅ kanajuq

sea ᑕᕆᐅᖅ tariuq

sea mammal ᐳᐃᔨ puiji

seagull ᓇᐅᔭᖅ naujaq

seal
(bearded) ᐅᔾᔪᒃ ujjuk
(harbour) ᖃᓯᒋᐊᖅ qasigiaq
(harp) ᖃᐃᕈᓕᒃ qairulik
(hooded) ᓇᑦᑎᕙᒃ nattivak
(ringed) ᓇᑦᑎᖅ nattiq

seal (he/she hunts)
ᓇᑦᑎᕋᓱᒋᐊᖅᑐᖅ nattirasugiaqtuq

seal flipper *(aged for eating)*
ᓯᖅᖁᖅ siqquq

seal skin ᕿᓯᒃ qisik

seashore ᐃᒪᐅᑉ ᓯᓈ imaup sinaa

seaweed *(frilly)* ᐃᖂᑎᑦ iquutit

seaweed *(long fern-like)*
ᑯᐊᓐᓃᖅ kuanniq

September ᓯᑎᐱᕆ sitipiri

seven ᓴᐃᐸᓐ saipan

seven *(traditional)*
ᓯᑕᒪᐅᔪᙱᒐᖅᑐᑦ
sitamaujunngigaqtut

sewing (I am)
ᒥᖅᓱᖅᑐᖓ miqsuqtunga

shed ᓯᕐᓗᐊᖅ sirluaq

shin ᑲᓈᒃ kanaak

shirt ᐃᑭᐊᖅᑎᖅ ikiaqtiq

shoes ᐃᓯᒐᐅᔮᒃ isigaujaak

shopping (I go)
ᓂᐅᕕᕆᐊᖅᑐᖓ niuviriaqtunga

short ᓇᐃᑦᑐᖅ naittuq

short hair ᓄᔭᑭᑦᑐᖅ nujakittuq

shoulder ᑐᐃ tui

shoulder blade ᑭᐊᓯᒃ kiasik

showering (I am)
ᐅᕕᓂᓐᓂᐊᖅᑐᖓ uvininniaqtunga

shy (I am feeling)
ᑲᙳᓱᑦᑐᖓ kanngusuttunga

sibling

(general)
ᖃᑕᙳᑎ qatannguti

(older of the same sex)
ᐊᖏᔪᒃ angijuk

(younger of same sex)
ᓄᑲᖅ nukaq

sick (I am) ᖃᓂᒪᔪᖓ qanimajunga

side *(of body)* ᓴᓂᕋᖅ saniraq

sinew ᐃᕙᓗ ivalu

singer ᐃᖏᖅᑎ inngiqti

sister *(of a male)*
ᓇᔭᒃ najak

six ᓴᔅᓯ sassi

six *(traditional)*
ᐱᖓᓲᔪᖅᑐᑦ pingasuujuqtut

skin
(human) ᐅᕕᓂᒃ uvinik
(land animals) ᐊᒥᖅ amiq
(sea mamals) ᕿᓯᒃ qisik

skin boots ᑲᒦᒃ kamiik

skin pants ᖃᕐᓕᑲᓪᓛᒃ qarlikallaak

skin tent ᐃᑦᑕᖅ ittaq

skirt ᐊᖏᔪᖅᑕᖅ angijuqtaq

sky ᕿᓚᒃ qilak

sled ᖃᒧᑏᒃ qamutiik

sleeping bag
ᐴᖅ; ᓯᓂᕝᕕᒃ puuq; sinivvik

sleepy (I am)
ᐅᐃᕐᙵᖅᑐᖓ uirngaqtunga

slow ᓱᒃᑲᐃᑦᑐᖅ sukkaittuq

small ᒥᑭᔪᖅ mikijuq

snaps *(clothing)*
ᓇᕿᑦᑕᖅᑐᖅ naqittaqtuq

snow

(general)
ᐊᐳᑦ aput

(becomes covered with snow)
ᐊᐱᔪᖅ apijuq

(drifting)
ᓇᑎᕈᕕᐊᖅᑐᖅ natiruviaqtuq

(hard packed)
ᑎᓯᓪᓗᖃᖅ tisilluqaq

(it is snowing)
ᖃᓐᓂᖅᑐᖅ qanniqtuq

(light dusting of)
ᐸᑑᑕᓕᒃ patuutalik

(mushy in springtime)
ᒪᙳᒪᔪᖅ mannguumajuq

(old, hard snow - like ice) ᐳᑲᔮᒃ pukajaak

(softens during the day & freezes at night in springtime)
ᕿᖅᓱᖅᑲᖓᔪᖅ qiqsuqqangajuq

(surface is iced up & hard)
ᓯᑯᕐᓚᒃ sikurlak

snow bunting
ᖁᐸᓄᐊᖅ qupanuaq

snow goose ᑲᖑᖅ kanguq

snow-covered
ᐊᐱᓯᒪᔪᖅ apisimajuq

snowmobile
ᖃᒧᑕᐅᔭᖅ qamutaujaq

snowmobile skis
ᓯᐊᕐᕆᔭᐅᑏᒃ siarrijautiik

snowmobiles (he/she)
ᖃᒧᑕᐅᔭᖅᑐᖅ qamutaujaqtuq

snowy owl ᐅᐱᒃ uppik

soft ᐊᕿᑦᑐᖅ aqittuq

sometimes ᐃᓛᓐᓂᒃᑯᑦ ilaannikkut

son ᐃᕐᓂᖅ irniq

soon ᖃᖓᑦᑎᐊᖅ qangattiaq

sorrel ᖁᖑᓖᑦ qunguliit

sorry ᒪᒥᐊᓇᖅ mamianaq

Sorry to hear it.
ᐅᒡᒍᐊᕐᓇᐅᒐᓗᐊᖅ
ugguarnaugaluaq

spine ᕿᒥᕐᓗᒃ qimirluk

spoon ᐊᓘᑦ aluut

spring ᐅᐱᕐᖔᖅ upirngaaq

stairs ᒪᔪᕋᐅᑎᑦ majurautit

stapler ᑭᑭᐊᑦᓯᔾᔪᑦ kikiatsijjut

star ᐅᓪᓗᕆᐊᖅ ulluriaq

stern (of a boat) ᐊᖁᐊ aqua

stew ᐊᒡᒍᐊᓚᕿᓵᖅ aggualaqisaaq

still *(motionless)*
ᓄᖅᑲᖓᔪᖅ nuqqangajuq

still *(unchanged)* ᓱᓕ suli

stomach ᓈᖅ naaq

stomach ache (I have a)
ᓈᙳᔪᖓ naanngujunga

Stop! ᓄᖅᑲᕆᑦ! Nuqqarit!

store ᓂᐅᕕᕐᕕᒃ niuvirvik

stormy weather
ᓱᓐᓇᐃᑦᑐᖅ sunnaittuq

stove ᐃᒐ iga

stove *(camping)* ᓲᐴᔪᖅ supuujuq

strait ᐃᑭᖅ ikiq

street ᐊᖅᑯᑦ aqqut

stumbles (he/she)
ᐹᓪᓚᒃᑐᖅ paallaktuq

sugar ᓱᑲᖅ sukaq

suit ᔭᐃᑲᒃᑕᕇᒃ jaikaktariik

summer ᐊᐅᔭᖅ aujaq

sun ᓯᕿᓂᖅ siqiniq

Sunday ᓈᑦᑏᙵᔭ naattiinguja

sunny (it is)
ᓯᕿᓐᓂᖅᑐᖅ siqinniqtuq

sunrise
ᓯᕿᓂᖅ ᓄᐃᔪᖅ siqiniq nuijuq

sunset
ᓯᕿᓂᖅ ᓂᐱᔪᖅ siqiniq nipijuq

sweater
ᓄᐃᔭᒐᖅ / ᖃᓕᐹᖅ
nuijagaq / qalipaaq

sweating (I am)
ᑭᐊᑦᑐᖓ kiattunga

T

table ᓵ saa

tall ᑕᑭᔪᖅ takijuq

Taloyoak ᑕᓗᕐᔪᐊᖅ Talurjuaq

taxi ᑖᑦᓯ taatsi

taxi (I call a)
ᑖᑦᓰᓕᕿᔪᖓ taatsiiliqijunga

tea ᑏ tii

tea (I am drinking)
ᑏᑐᖅᑐᖓ tiituqtunga

teacher ᐃᓕᓴᐃᔨ ilisaiji

telephone ᐅᖄᓚᐅᑦ uqaalaut

television (I am watching)
ᑕᓚᕖᓴᖅᑐᖓ talaviisaqtunga

ten ᖁᓕᑦ qulit

ten *(borrowed from English)*
ᑕᔭᓐ tajan

tendon ᐅᓕᐅᑏᒃ uliutiik

tent ᑐᐱᖅ tupiq

tent *(traditional made of skins)*
ᐃᑦᑕᖅ ittaq

tern ᐃᒥᖅᑯᑕᐃᓚᖅ imiqqutailaq

thank you
(Inuinnaqtun) ᖁᐊᓇ quana
(Kivalliq) ᒪ'ᓇ ma'na
(Baffin) ᖁᔭᓐᓇᒦᒃ qujannamiik
(S. Baffin) ᓇᑯᕐᒦᒃ nakurmiik

theirs (it is)
ᐅᓇ ᐱᖓᑦ. Una pingat.

There it is! ᑕᐃᑲ! Taika!

these ᐅᑯᐊ ukua

thigh ᖁᑦᑐᕋᖅ qutturaq

thirsty, are you? ᐃᒥᕈᑉᐱᑦ?
imiruppit?

this ᐅᓇ una

three ᐱᖓᓱᑦ pingasut

three *(borrowed from English)*
ᑕᓖ talii

thumb ᑯᓪᓗ kullu

Thursday ᓯᑕᒻᒥᖅ sitammiq

ticket (airline)
ᖃᖓᑦᑕᐅᑦ qangattaut

tide (high) ᐅᓕᑦᑐᖅ ulittuq

tide at full moon
ᐱᑐᕐᓂᕕᒃ piturnivik

tie for an amauti
ᖃᑦᓱᖓᐅᑦ qatsungaut

tie *(men's clothing)*
ᖁᖓᓯᕈᖅ qungasiruq

today ᐅᓪᓗᒥ ullumi

toe ᐳᑐᒍᖅ putuguq

tomorrow ᖃᐅᑉᐸᑦ qauppat

tongue ᐅᖃᖅ uqaq

tooth ᑭᒍᑎ kiguti

top of (it is on)
ᖄᖓᓃᑦᑐᖅ qaanganiittuq

traces *(dog team)* ᐃᐱᐅᑕᑦ ipiutat

tracks ᑐᒦᑦ tumiit

t-shirt ᐅᕕᓂᕈᖅ uviniruq

Tuesday ᐊᐃᑉᐱᖅ aippiq

turbot ᖃᓕᕋᓕᒃ qaliralik

twelve ᑐᐊᔪ tuaju

twenty ᐊᕙᑎᑦ avatit

twin (I have a)
ᒪᕐᕈᓕᐊᒥᓂᐅᖃᑎᖃᖅᑐᖓ
marruliaminiuqatiqaqtunga

two ᒪᕐᕉᒃ marruuk

two *(borrowed from English)* ᑑ tuu

U

unbelievable (it is)
ᐅᐱᕐᓇᖏᑦᑐᖅ uppirnangittuq

uncooked food
ᐆᓯᒪᙱᑦᑐᑦ uusimanngittut

underneath (it is)
ᐊᑖᓃᑦᑐᖅ ataaniittuq

us ᐅᕙᒍᑦ uvagut

V

vagina ᐅᑦᓲᒃ utsuuk

valley ᓇᖅᓴᖅ naqsaq

vest ᐅᐊᓯᑯᐊᖅ uasikuaq

visitor (I have a)
ᐳᓛᖅᑎᖃᖅᑐᖓ
pulaaqtiqaqtunga

W

waist ᕿᑎᖅ qitiq

waiter ᐱᔨᑲᑖᖅ pijikataaq

wake up (I) ᑐᐸᑦᑐᖓ tupattunga

walks (he/she) ᐱᓱᒃᑐᖅ pisuktuq

wall ᐊᕙᓗ avalu

wall hanging
ᐊᕙᓗᒥᐅᑕᖅ avalumiutaq

walrus ᐊᐃᕕᖅ aiviq

walrus meat *(fermented)*
ᐃᒍᓇᖅ igunaq

warm weather ᐅᖅᑰᔪᖅ uqquujuq

washroom ᐊᓇᕐᕕᒃ anarvik

Watch out!
ᖃᐅᔨᒪᒋᐊᕆᑦ! Qaujimagiarit!

water
(for drinking) ᐃᒥᖅ imiq
(an expanse of) ᐃᒪᖅ imaq

water's edge *(land/ice)* ᓯᔾᔭ sijja

waterfall ᖁᕐᓗᕐᓂᖅ qurlurniq

wavy ᒪᓪᓕᖅᑐᖅ malliqtuq

we ᐅᕙᒍᑦ uvagut

weasel ᑎᕆᐊᖅ tiriaq

weather ᓯᓚ sila

Wednesday ᐱᖓᑦᓯᖅ pingatsiq

week ᐱᓇᓱᐊᕈᓯᖅ pinasuarusiq

welcome *(speaking to 1 person)*
ᑐᙵᓱᒋᑦ tunngasugit

welcome (you're) ᐃᓛᓕ ilaali

wet ᖃᐅᓯᖅᑐᖅ qausiqtuq

whale (he/she catches)
ᕿᓚᓗᒐᖅᑐᖅ qilalugaqtuq

whale (he/she hunts)
ᕿᓚᓗᒃᑭᐊᖅᑐᖅ qilalukkiaqtuq

Whale Cove ᑎᑭᕋᕐᔪᐊᖅ Tikirarjuaq

whale vertebrae ᑯᔭᐱᒐᖅ kujapigaq

What are these?
ᐅᑯᐊ ᑭᓲᕙᑦ? Ukua kisuuvat?

What are you doing? ᓱᕕᑦ? suvit?

What did he/she say?
ᓱᕙᒎᖅ? suvaguuq?

What did you say?
ᓱᕙ?; Hᐊᐃ? suva?; hai?

mini-dictionary : english - inuktitut

What do you think?
ᖃᓄᕐᓕ ᐃᓱᒪᕕᑦ Qanurli isumavit?

What is his / her name?
ᑭᓇᐅᕙ? kinauva?

What is this?
ᐅᓇ ᑭᓲᕙ? Una kisuuva?

What time? *(will something happen)*
ᖃᑦᑎᒨᖅᑲᑦ? qattimuuqqat?

What time is it?
ᖃᑦᑎᒨᖅᐸ? qattimuuqpa?

What's your name?
ᑭᓇᐅᕕᑦ? kinauvit?

when? ᖃᖓ? qanga?

Where are you from?
ᓇᒥᒥᐅᑕᐅᕕᑦ? namimiutauvit?

Where are you going?
ᓇᒧᙵᖅᐱᑦ? namunngaqpit?

Where are you originally from?
ᓇᒥᒥᐅᔅᓴᔭᐅᕕᑦ? namimiussajauvit?

Where do you live?
ᓇᒥᒥᐅᑕᐅᕕᑦ? namimiutauvit?

Where is it? ᓇᒦᑉᐸ? namiippa?

where? ᓇᒥ? nami?

while (in a) ᒫᓐᓇᕈᓗᒃ maannaruluk

whip *(dog team)* ᐃᐸᕋᐅᑦ iparaut

white ᖃᑯᖅᑐᖅ qakuqtuq

white hair ᖀᖅ qiiq

whitecaps ᖃᒑᖅᑐᖅ qagaaqtuq

who? ᑭᓇ? kina

why? ᓱᒻᒪᑦ? summat?

wife ᓄᓕᐊᖅ nuliaq

wind ᐊᓄᕆ anuri

wind pants ᖃᕐᓕᐊᓘᒃ qarlialuuk

window ᐃᒐᓛᖅ igalaaq

windy (it is) ᐊᓄᕌᖅᑐᖅ anuraaqtuq

wine ᕙᐃᓂ vaini

winter ᐅᑭᐅᖅ ukiuq

winter boots
ᑲᒫᓘᒃ ᐅᑭᐅᖅᓯᐅᑏᒃ
kamaaluuk ukiuqsiutiik

wolf ᐊᒪᕈᖅ amaruq

wolf tracks
ᐊᒪᕈᕐᒧᑦ ᑐᒦᑦ amarurmut tumiit

wolverine ᖃᕝᕕᒃ qavvik

wolverine fur ᖃᕝᕕᕋᔭᒃ qavvirajak

wonderful (it is)
ᐊᓕᐊᓇᐃᑦ alianait

works (he/she)
ᐃᖅᑲᓇᐃᔭᖅᑐᖅ iqqanaijaqtuq

wrist ᐸᕝᕕᒃ pavvik

wrist watch ᑕᓕᐊᖅ taliaq

Y

year ᐊᕐᕌᒍ arraagu

yellow ᖁᖅᓱᖅᑐᖅ quqsuqtuq

yes ᐄ ii

yesterday ᐃᑉᐸᔅᓴᖅ ippassaq

you
(1 person) ᐃᕝᕕᑦ ivvit
(2 people) ᐃᓕᑦᓯᒃ ilitsik
(3 +) ᐃᓕᑦᓯ ilitsi

younger sibling *(of same sex)*
ᓄᑲᖅ nukaq

Z

zero ᔨᐅᓗ jiulu

zipper ᓯᖀᖅ siqiiq

ᐱᕿᕐᕕᒃ

also from Pirurvik

Pirurvik supports Inuktitut learning through productions of the highest quality in print, music and on the internet.

Pigiarvik: An introduction to Inuktitut

The first in our series of handbooks for Inuktitut learners. *Pigiarvik* includes vocabulary lists, dialogues built around real-life situations, and grammar notes that explain how Inuktitut speakers build words and sentences. 96 pages.

Allurvik: The Next Step to Learning Inuktitut

For those who are ready to take the next step toward fluency. *Allurvik* provides more advanced vocabulary, dialogues, grammar notes and practice exercises.
112 pages.

Inuttaqalauqpuq

Leena Evic's popular CD of children's music includes both traditional Inuktitut songs and those adapted from English classics.

Surusiqsiutit Inngiutit (Inuktitut songbook for children)

This book provides lyrics to dozens of Inuktitut songs including all those that appear on Leena Evic's CD, *Inuttaqalauqpuq.*
94 pages.

tusaalanga.ca

The most popular website anywhere for the learning of Inuktitut. Tusaalanga includes 20 lessons, over 1,000 vocabulary items with French and English translations, dialogues with soundfiles and practice exercises.